H.M. WYNANT:
YOU MUST BELIEVE!

STEVEN PEROS

FOREWORD BY ALAN K. RODE

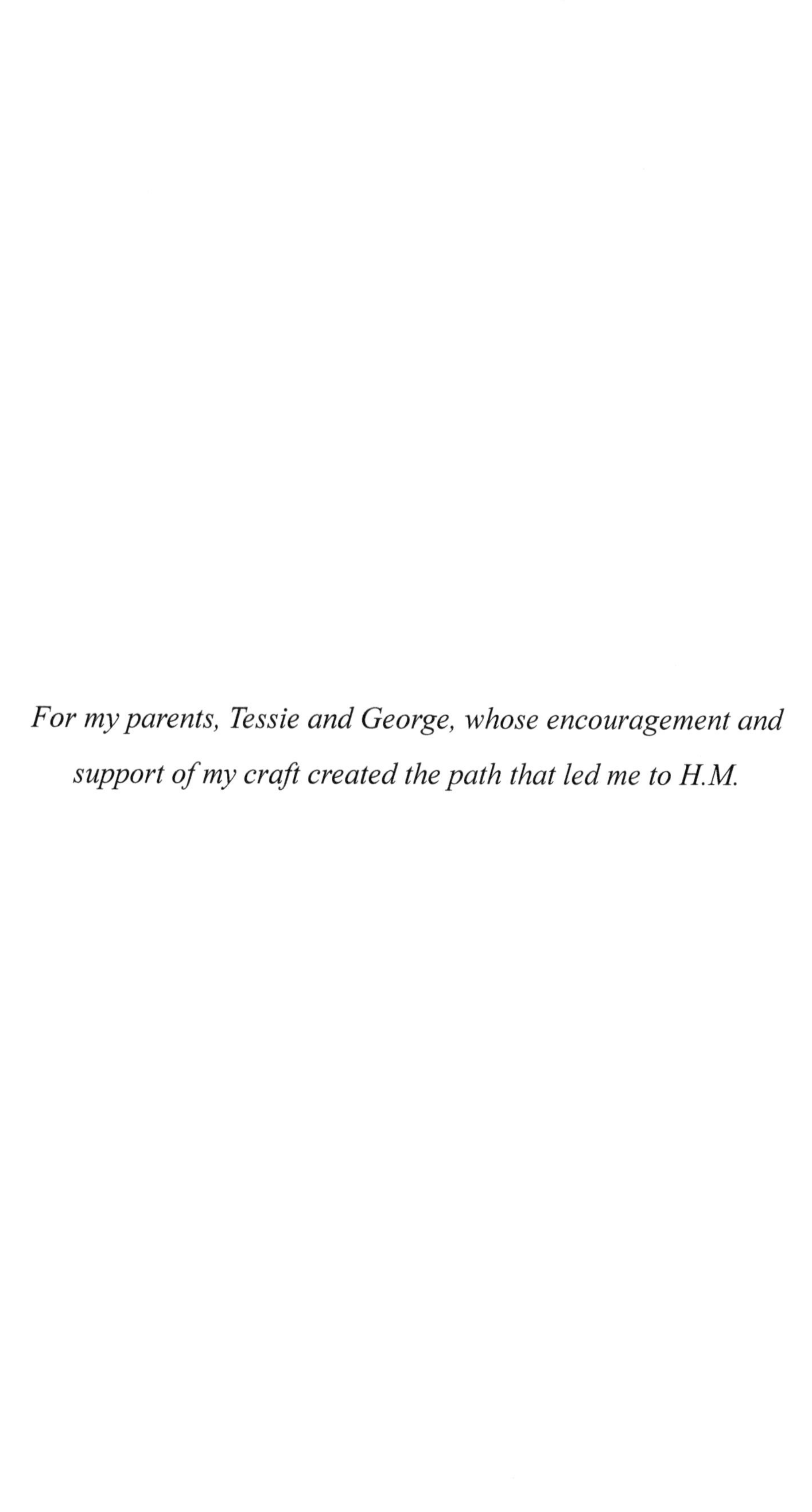

For my parents, Tessie and George, whose encouragement and support of my craft created the path that led me to H.M.

H.M. WYNANT: YOU MUST BELIEVE!

©2024 Steven Peros

All rights reserved.

No part of this book may be reproduced in any form or by any means, electronic, mechanical, digital, photocopying, or recording, except for inclusion of a review, without permission in writing from the publisher.

Published in the USA by:

BearManor Media
1317 Edgewater Dr. #110
Orlando FL 32804
www.BearManorMedia.com

ISBN-10: 979-8-88771-574-2 H.M. Wynant
ISBN-13: 979-8-88771-575-9 H.M. Wynant hb

All photos from the author's and H.M. Wynant's personal collection

Art, Design, and Layout: Steven Peros and Mark Bailey

Table of Contents

Foreword

The late Jack Elam aptly defined the life cycle of a Hollywood character actor: "Who's Jack Elam? Get me Jack Elam. Get me a Jack Elam type. Get me a young Jack Elam. Who's Jack Elam?"

Replacing Elam's name with that of H.M. Wynant is a spot-on description of a nearly eight decade career in films and television begun when Jerome Robbins plucked the twenty-year-old dancer from 60 tryouts and cast him in the Broadway musical *High Button Shoes* in 1947.

It wasn't an easy journey for Haim Weiner, born into a musical family in Detroit. Excelling with a pool cue instead of schoolbooks, dance became his passion with acting his career inflection point.

Leaving the company of *Guys and Dolls*, Wynant (who changed his name after arriving in New York with $125 in his pocket and no prospects) became the assistant stage manager for a production of *As You Like It* starring Katharine Hepburn. He was done with dancing, became an actor, and never looked back.

After more plays and early live television in New York, he relocated to Hollywood in 1956 and has never left. Haim Wynant never aspired to be a movie star. The work was the thing. He turned down next to nothing as his face and voice became familiar to millions via countless television programs and movies. Wynant worked with nearly every movie star and prominent actor for the next half century while maintaining his equilibrium though three marriages and four children.

Although Steven Peros wrote this biography as a valentine to his close friend of thirty years, he doesn't pull any punches. The accounts of Wynant's personal life and career ups and downs are unremittingly honest. What comes through is the fascinating narrative of an actor's life in a Hollywood that sadly no longer exists.

For those who are not familiar with the life of a working actor spanning the veritable history of television, there is enlightenment within these pages. As Wynant himself put it, acting was a *job*. Personally, I'm delighted that he always said "yes" to a gig when his agent phoned. I'm even happier that Steven Peros took the time to write this joyous book about a master actor who brought an incredible amount of professionalism and craft to every one of his performances. Bravo!

by Alan K. Rode
Author of *Michael Curtiz: A Life in Film,*
Charles McGraw: Film Noir Tough Guy, and *Blood on the Moon*

Introduction & Acknowledgements

I have known H.M. Wynant for thirty years. As you will learn in the pages ahead, we met through work when I was referred to him in 1994 to play the lead in my original stage play, *Karlaboy*. In the years since, we have become friends, then close pals, and now, in many ways, family.

Since you are reading this book, you probably already know who H.M. Wynant is. His career as a professional actor on Broadway and in Hollywood has spanned eight decades. Read that again slowly:

Eight. Decades.

But you will soon learn that unlike many biographies, this is also for anyone who may not know H.M. by name but wants to know, experience, and *feel* what it was like to be barely twenty years old in Manhattan in the late 1940's and early 1950's, performing on Broadway every night, dancing Jerome Robbins' choreography in his very first show, appearing on stage with Laurence Olivier, Phil Silvers, Rex Harrison, and Katharine Hepburn, while running to television studios in the daytime during the dawn of live TV dramas, to work with the likes of Charlton Heston and Boris Karloff.

It's a book for anyone who wants to know what it was like to be not yet thirty-years-old and recruited to come out to Hollywood in the mid-1950's to not only appear in movies with Clark Gable, Burt Lancaster, Charles Bronson, and Rod Steiger, but to have juicy guest roles on quite literally all of the most famous TV dramas and Westerns (and a few of the comedies) on the air from the 1950's through the 1970's, as well as live TV dramas with George C. Scott, Mickey Rooney, Ricardo Montalban, and Jack Warden. And of course, starring in a little piece of TV history called *The Twilight Zone*, a line of dialogue from which the title of this book is derived.

When I first embarked on writing H.M.'s jaw-dropping story, I thought it would be in memoir form with an authorship akin to "by H.M. Wynant, as told to Steven Peros". But that soon shifted as it became clear to both of us that I would be interviewing him for an authorized biography of my writing, quoting him throughout.

As a close friend to the subject, there may be the assumption that what follows will be a puff piece. Such is not the case. Not only am I candid about H.M.'s career and life choices, but far more importantly, so was H.M. during our interviews. In fact, it was H.M.'s candor that provided the encouragement I needed to assess his story honestly and put it into context.

H.M. has survived to 97 years old as of this writing not only through excellent genes (longevity runs in his family), but because he has always looked situations directly in the eye, one day at a time, dealt with them, and moved on without regret. He's done so throughout his life and career, and he did so during our interviews for this book. This pragmatism has not only been a Zen-like strength throughout H.M.'s life, but one could argue it was sometimes a weakness in terms of career, when he could have been more ambitious, taken more risks, and/or sought loftier goals.

But as H.M. has said repeatedly, and the facts bear him out, he was never trying to be a star, just a working character actor, much to the consternation of his early agents who imagined him reaching movie star heights, which sometimes comes from saying No as opposed to Yes. As the son of working-class immigrants from a poor area of Detroit, saying no to work is just not in H.M.'s instruction manual.

As I interviewed H.M., it became evident that there were areas where his memory was not so clear, particularly regarding films and TV shows from fifty or sixty years ago. This is less due to advancing years than the fact that these classic TV shows and movies, which have made such an impact on our lives, often only amounted to two or three days of work to him, after which they were disposed of from his memory banks in order to move on to the next job. You try recalling two or three days of work from last year, let alone five decades ago. Good luck!

Because of this, I am thankful that H.M. has given interviews to others over the years. I would like to acknowledge the following for the use of quotes from their interviews with H.M.: Tom & Jim Goldrup's interview in the mid-1990's (*The Encyclopedia of Hollywood, Vol. 3*), Andrew Ramage for his 2004 interview at the "Stars of the Twilight Zone" convention (as printed in *The Twilight Zone Encyclopedia* by Steven Jay Rubin), Frank Dietz, Scott Weitz, Trish Geiger, and Michael Schlesinger for their 2017 interview with H.M. on their *Damn Dirty Geeks* podcast, Rob Word and his *Word on Westerns* interview conducted in 2018 at the Gene Autry Museum, and Stu Shostack for his 2014 interview with H.M. on *Stu's Show*.

I would also like to acknowledge and personally thank the entire Wynant/Winant family, particularly, H.M.'s wife, Paula, youngest son Bruce, daughter Pasha, and niece Shelley Weiner Flannery (daughter of H.M.'s eldest brother, Max) for always being available to me for questions throughout the process and for furnishing me with many of the personal photos found in this book.

My gratitude extends, of course, to Ben Ohmert at Bear-Manor Media for recognizing the historical importance of this book from the start and wholeheartedly supporting it. Along the way, others have been of aid: Steven Orkin for his peerless copy editing and suggestions, which improved this book immensely, Mark Bailey for his stellar design, Cary O'Dell, in researching a program that could only be viewed in person at the Library of Congress; Phoef Sutton, Justin Humphreys for their feedback to my first draft (and Justin, additionally, for his aid with photos), Alan Rode for his corrections and lovely foreword, my big brother Mike (a biographer in his own right) for his thoughts and advice, my brother, John, who has given his support on this and other projects in countless ways, and my girlfriend, Deana Ruggieri, for giving me the room, the love, and the confidence to write this book, her additional proofreading, and for being kind enough to vacuum around me and make sure I stayed hydrated throughout the process.

And finally, my indebtedness to H.M. for trusting me to tell his tale, a responsibility I did not take lightly. His honesty, fearlessness, and ability to see the truth in his life story is something I was in awe of throughout the process. You're in for quite a ride, as he was, so don't blink for a moment or you might miss something.

Weiner family portrait in Detroit, circa 1931. From left: Malka ("Mollie"), Pesha ("Bessie"), Yakov ("Jack"), Munya ("Max"), Chaya ("Charlie"), and H.M., then Hyman ("Haim").

Chapter One

Bad Boy in Detroit (1927-1945)

"I was sort of a bad kid. I failed terribly in school.
Hung out at the pool hall. My family was very worried about me.
I was about fifteen years old.
But at sixteen, I picked up Shakespeare
and it changed my life."

That revelatory moment for H.M. Wynant occurred in 1943. The place: Detroit. In those years, H.M. was known as "Haim" but was actually born Hyman Oscar Weiner on February 12, 1927, the only child born in the U.S. to Polish Jews, Yakov ("Jack") and Pesha ("Bessie") Weiner. The first language of the Weiner household was Yiddish and H.M.'s birth-name of Hyman was the Yiddish altered form of the Hebrew name, "Hyam" or "Chaim", meaning "Life".

In 1926, Jack and Bessie emigrated to Detroit, Michigan from the Poland/Austria border town of Kolomay. With them were H.M.'s three older siblings, all born three years apart and all given new "Americanized" names at New York's Ellis Island: Malka ("Mollie"), Munya ("Max"), and Chaya ("Charlie"). The Weiners entered the U.S., sponsored by Bessie's sister, who lived in Detroit. Within a year, Haim was born, their youngest.

"My first language was Yiddish, which is all I spoke until

the age of four or five," H.M. recalled. "Both of my parents went to night school to learn English and become citizens. Dad played the violin and had his own Klezmer band. Three to five members. His music was the Jewish music."

"It was a Jewish family like we don't have any more. Mother in charge of everything. The father laid back — on cushions! That's the way it was. The male of the family was always in a relaxed position."

"Mom was the Number 2 cook and dishwasher in kosher kitchens. She did Bar Mitzvahs, weddings. She was unbelievably self-educated. She spoke six languages, but you'd never know it. She was just a Jewish mom. Because of how much mom worked, my sister Mollie, who was nine years older than me, brought me up. She was my second mother. Mollie was more my mother than my mother."

"We were a musical family. Dad made us all learn instruments. On weekends, the house was full of musicians. My brother, Max, played the violin and had a little orchestra. When he was away, I took charge. I actually conducted. That's when I found out I couldn't conduct. I thought you just had to wave a stick."

"Charlie played all the instruments. He was the real, genuine musician among all of us. Later, he became a high school teacher."

But it was brother Max who had the drive and made a career from his "fiddle", playing violin in the Detroit Symphony Orchestra, then the Chicago Symphony, and finally "the ultimate orchestra", recalled H.M., "The New York Philharmonic, where he played for several decades before retiring."

"I was not good with the fiddle," remembered H.M. "Then I picked up the trumpet and I liked it. I played with the Detroit Symphony Orchestra for a short time."

Ultimately, it was not the family tradition of instrument-playing that proved to be young Haim's musical passion, but dance. "My first classical ballet teacher in Detroit was an old man, Mr. Smith. He was on a crutch, for Christ's sake. He couldn't move! But he was a great teacher. I went through the Cecchetti Method[1] and finished all five stages."

"I had Mr. Smith for over a year, five days a week. I was self-motivated and became a fucking good dancer. I began studying in my late teens, not as a child. I only had one problem. My arms were weak, so I was bad with lifts, especially bringing them down slowly. But I could do a marvelous *Entrechat Six*!"

Although excelling as a dancer, young Haim was not doing well in school. It wasn't until years later that he realized he was

[1]The Cecchetti method is a ballet technique devised by the Italian ballet master Enrico Cecchetti (1850–1928). The method seeks to develop the essential skills of dance (e.g., balance, poise, strength, elevation, flexibility, and artistry) in ballet students.

Weiner siblings, circa 1943. From left: Haim, Max, Mollie, Charlie.

dyslexic. "It was not a word you heard back then," remembered H.M. "I just knew I was backwards."

"I was extremely dyslexic, which no one knew about. I couldn't read or write, which is why I failed everything. I was in trouble in high school and hid from it by hanging out at the local pool room when I was still underage."

By H.M.'s account, the Jewish neighborhood where he and his family lived was "a bad neighborhood called 12th & Clairmount. We lived in a two-story house on Gladstone and right next door was an apartment building where my Aunt lived (his mother's sister). Three blocks away was a big pool hall on the corner. I was an excellent pool player as a kid and beat the older guys, who all liked me. I was a better pool player than anybody there, practically. The pool hall was raided every once in a while and they would hide me in the toilet." Twenty-one years after Haim's departure, his neighborhood would be the center of the historic 1967 Detroit race riots.

But it was Haim's first exposure to stage plays at age sixteen that would set him on the course he would take for the rest of his life. "I picked up Shakespeare and it changed my life. I don't know why I was reading it, or how I was able to read it, but I did."

From that point forward, Haim's life in Detroit was spent between two theatrical disciplines: Dance and Acting. He began to establish his performing chops by teaming with a dancer in his class and forming a Spanish Dance couple called, "Carl & Carmelita". They played in small venues for little or no pay, such as Veterans Hospitals.

To further his studies, Haim became a non-matriculated student at Wayne University's Speech Department, which today would be called the Communications Department. Wayne's recently instituted Radio program was popular at the time, which led Haim to hone his acting skills as a radio actor for the college-produced, "Book Spring Adventures", a one-hour live radio show, every week. "It was mostly adaptations of great books," H.M. recalled. The college radio station, WSC, provided programming to

WJAG in Norfolk, Nebraska, three states west, which at the time was owned by the Norfolk Daily News. This training became particularly useful for the countless live TV dramas in which Haim would ultimately perform in Manhattan and, later, in Los Angeles.

But after one-and-a-half years at Wayne University, Haim was feeling there was nothing left for him to learn in Detroit, so he dropped out of college. It was clear to him that if he was serious about being a dancer, he needed to go where the serious dancers go — Manhattan.

"In 1946, at age nineteen, I was looking for a life. I had no life. I had nothing. No girlfriend. I really had no social life. I had to go to New York to become a dancer because that's where the great teachers are. That's what I wanted to be. I kept talking about it with my family but kept being ignored. So one day, I packed a suitcase. They knew I was going but nobody was there to say goodbye. I was very sad. I left my keys, went out the door, and went to the train station with $125 I had saved up."

"I bought a one-way ticket to New York."

Chapter Two

BROADWAY BABY (1946-1950)

Jerome Robbins, Phil Silvers, and Katharine Hepburn
… just for starters.

"I came to New York to become a dancer, not an actor."

Upon getting off the train in Manhattan, H.M. recalled, "I knew nobody! The first place I went was the YMCA on 34th Street. I had traveled on the train from Detroit with a casual friend, a would-be actor. We weren't close, but we both wanted to go to New York. We got a double room at the YMCA. Two beds. He got in his bed, I got in my bed. We turned the lights out to go to sleep and then the door was suddenly thrown wide open, the lights go on, and three or four guys look and see we're in our own beds. They were expecting us to be homosexuals but when we were in our own beds, they just left."

As Haim began to hit the Manhattan pavement, looking for work as a dancer, the first of his two name changes occurred. "My own ego changed my name from

First professional Broadway headshot, age 19.

Weiner to Winant. I knew it was too 'ethnic'. My own choice. I went to a numerologist and that's where I got Winant from. Haim was unique, so I let that be. Back then, you didn't have to do anything legal. You just changed your name and it becomes legal. You went to the DMV back then, you correct their spelling, and they just accepted it."

But his $125 was running out fast. As H.M. recalled, "Ross Martin, Jack Lemmon, and I used to hang out at Cromwell's Drugstore at 30 Rock. We read the magazines and put them back. We all had no money!" Haim realized he had to take any job he could find if he was going to stay in Manhattan, and so he got a job as a shoe salesman. After his first day of work, he answered yet another open call for dancers at the New Century Theatre on Seventh Avenue and 58th Street (demolished in 1962).

"Audition notices were posted on the stage door and the line for auditions went around the block." It was an open call for a new musical called *High Button Shoes* and its pedigree was the stuff of legend: music by Jule Styne, lyrics by Sammy Cahn, directed by George Abbott. But Haim was auditioning for its choreographer, who would ultimately win the first of his five Tony Awards for his work on the show: Jerome Robbins.

After an exhausting all-day audition process, Haim was one of sixty remaining dancers. Jerome Robbins pointed to a handful, including Haim: "You, you, and you, come back tomorrow." Tomorrow would be the callback when Robbins would make his final choices for the show's coveted dance ensemble.

As the others packed up to leave the theater, Haim approached Robbins confidentially, "I can't come back tomorrow because I have a job."

"In what show?" Robbins asked.

"Not a show. A straight job at a shoe store."

Robbins considered this, looked Haim up and down, came close to his face, and said, "Quit."

As H.M. explained, "I quit the shoe store job after one day and have never had a straight job since." The demands of being in the dance chorus of a major Broadway show was indeed the baptism-by-fire that Haim had dreamed about when he had gotten on that train in Detroit less than a year before. And nothing could test the commitment and determination of a twenty-year-old dancer like the blister-bleeding perfectionism of Jerome Robbins.

"During rehearsals, Jerry Robbins was unbelievably mean to me. He would curse me out. 'You stop dancing before you're off stage!' He'd yell at me constantly. Fired me every other day. I felt so defeated. I even cried."

But then, Maria Karnilova, the Dance Leader, took Haim aside. At 27, Karnilova had made her Broadway debut only one year earlier. Eighteen years later, she'd win the Tony for originating the role of "Golde" in *Fiddler on the Roof*, opposite Zero Mostel.

In the wings, Karnilova asked the distraught Haim, "Don't you know why he treats you like that?"

Haim shook his head sadly, fearing it was because he wasn't good enough.

"He yells at you," she began, "because he loves you."

Looking back, H.M. recalled, "That was my first exposure to homosexuality. I didn't understand it at all, but he was in love with me. Then it all made sense."

Ultimately, Haim would be part of the original cast of *High Button Shoes* as a Lead Dancer in the very active dance company, which also had to engage in choreographed, Mack Sennett, Keystone Cops-style comic hijinks.

Soon Haim became so confident that he actually created a piece of choreography: "It was a scene coming out of the bathing room doors at the beach. I came out of my door, I ran to the footlights. That's where I was supposed to stop and do a little circular thing jumping over my leg. But I didn't. What I did was I jumped, full jete, out into the audience, to the first row. Everyone ducked, but then I withdrew my leg and landed on the footlights. Scared the shit out of everyone, including Jerry Robbins, but they left it in. I did it every night."

The show was a hit, opening at the New Century Theatre on October 9, 1947 and transferring to the Shubert on December 22 where it ran for ten more months into 1948.

Although the final stop of its 727-performance run would be at the Broadway Theatre (where it closed on July 2, 1949), Haim was sent off on the National Tour in 1948, which ran parallel to the Broadway run. This resulted in a thrilling turn of events for Haim because he not only understudied "Uncle Willie", but ultimately took over the role halfway through the tour.

For the tour, the starring role originated by rising comedy genius, Phil Silvers, was taken over by Broadway veteran, Eddie Foy, Jr., who H.M. found much more embracing. "Phil

As part of the show-stopping Keystone Cops ensemble in *High Button Shoes*.

Silvers was very aloof. He's not 'one of the people'. A very funny man, but kept to himself. He went right to his dressing room and closed the door. Which means nobody comes in."

Another plus of going on an 85-week tour for young Haim was the chance to become close with its 26-year-old touring star, Audrey Meadows, who had taken on the role being played on Broadway by Nanette Fabray. "Audrey Meadows was The Lady in the Red Gown, who I loved. Literally. I was truly in love with her for a while. In my eyes, she was the most beautiful thing in the world. We spent a lot of time together. We did a soft shoe number

H.M.'s personal *High Button Shoes* backstage photo
with his own markings, identifying who's who.

in the show. We weren't a big thing, but we came very close. After the show, I taught her a dance for a big audition she had coming up. Her big sister, Jane Meadows, arranged it. Jane was like the mama to her. I taught Audrey the steps, but she couldn't do it. So, I did it in front of her, behind the camera, and she mimicked me. A soft-shoe routine. She got the job, which was with Jackie Gleason, and eventually led to *The Honeymooners*."

Upon concluding his successful Broadway dancing debut - the very thing Haim came to New York to achieve - Haim made his first appearance on a movie screen, albeit uncredited, in the notorious cult favorite, *So Young, So Bad* (1950) starring *Casablanca*'s Paul Henreid as a psychiatrist who, with the help of a nurse, exposes the abuses going on at a girls' reformatory. Released by United Artists, it was shot independently on locations in Manhattan and Long Island in July of 1949 by the resourceful sibling producing team of Edward and Harry Danziger. Haim (then 22) appeared in the movie at a chaperoned dance scene between the reform school girls and the local boys. Clearly Haim was hired for his dance experience because at the 1:08 mark, he is the camera's focal point as he dances across screen (inarguably with more balletic grace than the average schoolboy), flawlessly flashing a thousand-watt smile toward the camera as he does so. For a young man who initially came to Manhattan to be a dancer, *So Young, So Bad* is the only instance of H.M. dancing professionally captured on film.

That reliable dance experience would lead him to be cast in the dance company of a new show going into rehearsals on Broadway called *Guys and Dolls*. But something was unsettled in Haim. His time on stage as *High Button Shoe's* "Uncle Willie" opened him up to the possibility that he could take on more substantial acting roles. He was eased into the process by a system little known to the layman: the job of Assistant Stage Manager. The position, chosen by the Stage Manager, is nearly always filled by an actor, the reason being that their key function is to be in the wings, on book, so they can throw an actor their line should they forget (or "go up on a line", per common theater lingo). Since the Assistant Stage Manager becomes so familiar with the script and blocking, they are the perfect choice to understudy numerous roles, stepping in when necessary, which was the case in Haim's second Broadway show.

When the opportunity presented itself to do some straight acting, Haim left *Guys and Dolls* during rehearsals to accept an offer from much sought-after Stage Manager Karl Nielsen to be his Assistant Stage Manager. It was yet another landmark Broadway production: Shakespeare's *As You Like It* starring Katharine Hepburn.

As H.M. clarified, "From that point on, I never danced

again and became only an actor."

Regarding the Assistant Stage Manager's key function to throw an actor a line should they go up, H.M. explained, "The actors never used me! Never! But if they didn't see you in the wings, they panicked. All they had to do was see you and they knew things would be fine."

Directed by Englishman, Michael Benthall, *As You Like It* opened at the Cort Theatre on January 26, 1950, just two-and-a-half weeks shy of Haim's 23rd birthday. At 145 performances, it became the longest running Broadway production of the play until it was unseated 36 years later by Joe Papp's production at the Belasco. Along with being Assistant Stage Manager, Haim understudied the role of "Dennis, Servant to Oliver", which he eventually took over when he joined Hepburn on the National Tour shortly after it closed at the Cort on June 3, 1950.

"Katharine and I used to play tennis when we were on the road. In fact, she borrowed my tennis clothes! She was a creature of habit and had the same meal every day: a small steak and a baked potato. We became close. Harvey Korman and I never appeared in anything together, but we were friends and the same age - he was three days younger than me. He always thought I was having an affair with Hepburn. Of course I didn't, but I always sort of let him believe it."

"Hepburn was among the biggest stars but never behaved like that. She behaved like one of us. She was a friend. Not a superior of any kind, just one of us. She made it easy. I ran into her long after we closed, in Los Angeles, in a pharmacy. I was so in shock that I clammed up."

Also in the cast was English acting legend, Ernest Thesiger, who will forever be remembered for his role as Doctor Pretorious in *The Bride of Frankenstein* (1935). "I loved Ernest Thesiger. He was 71 but he looked 100! We're all there, all the Merry Men, and then he comes on 'A fool! A fool! I met a fool in the forest!' That was his first line. I'll never forget it."

"After it closed, Hepburn recommended me to Irene Selznick who was producing *Bell, Book and Candle*. Irene sent her assistant, Ethel Wald, to find me. I didn't get the role, but I did get a wife."

Portrait taken in New York of H.M. performing the ballet, *Specter of the Rose*, **circa 1949.**

Chapter Three

THE ACTOR EMERGES (1950-1953)

Directed by Olivier, on stage with Rex Harrison — twice!

"I've always felt more comfortable acting than not acting, 100%. I want to be someone else. Always."

Ethel Wald was born in Massachusetts in 1922 but raised in rural Marysville, California. After the death of her father (a World War 1 veteran who had a host of war-induced medical issues), her mother relocated to California where she fought to get a job at the California Division of Highways. She was a tenacious, independent woman who raised a tenacious, independent daughter.

Ethel went to UC Berkley to study liberal arts and then on to Whittier College where she got her Masters in Theater. Along the way, she studied at the Pasadena Playhouse, finding herself gravitating less towards acting and more on how a great production is put together.

Just as Haim knew he had to go to New York if he was serious about Dance, so too did Ethel make a similar move from California to Manhattan to find work in the Theater. A series of jobs led her to work as an assistant to Broadway producer, Irene Selznick, the daughter of MGM founder Louis B. Mayer and wife of famed producer David O. Selznick (from whom she was getting divorced). Ethel began her Broadway career on the set of *A Streetcar Named Desire*, which Selznick produced, assisting star Marlon Brando, director Elia Kazan, and its author, Tennessee Williams.

The next production on which Ethel assisted Selznick was the comedy, *Bell, Book and Candle*, starring husband and wife, Rex Harrison and Lilli Palmer. When Selznick voiced the trouble she was having casting the role of "Nicky" to her friend Katharine Hepburn, the actress recommended she take a look at Haim Winant, who had so impressed her in *As You Like It*, and which had just completed its National Tour. Selznick instructed Ethel to track down Haim. The role ultimately went to Scott McKay, but resulted in Haim and Ethel beginning a romantic relationship.

Two days after *As You Like It* closed at the Cort, just before going on tour with Hepburn, Haim landed the first of two "firsts": his first appearance on television in *Studio One*'s modern dress, one-hour, live adaptation of *The Taming of the Shrew*, starring Charlton Heston as Petruchio, which aired live on June 5, 1950. Haim (billed under his birth name of "Haim Weiner") played Curtis, Servant to Petruchio.

"We rehearsed for eighty hours or more," explained H.M. "I think Chuck Heston got about one hundred and twenty dollars and I made forty or sixty. That was before the unions, and then we created a little union called TVA (Television Authority) which had no power, and that eventually merged in 1952 with AFRA (American Federation of Radio Artists) and became AFTRA."[2]

The second "first" was his first role in a non-musical Broadway play, *Never Say Never*, opposite Anne Jackson. Prior to this, Haim's Broadway speaking parts were roles he had understudied that resulted in being cast. Now, in *Never Say Never* by Carl Leo, Haim was in the Opening Night cast.

"I loved Anne," H.M. remembered. "She was a wonderful lady. All I can say is… we were very good friends all through the rehearsal period." Jackson had been married to Eli Wallach for over two years when she and Haim met, which is why H.M. hesitated to elaborate on any further details of his warm backstage relationship with her. Throughout H.M.'s eight-decade career, he would have romantic affairs, both minor and major, but was only willing to go on record if he was the only one of the two who was being unfaithful. In other words, if he was married at the time of the liaison, he had no qualms discussing the clandestine romance. But if the woman was married, he preferred not to go on record, out of respect.

According to the New York Times announcing the opening of *Never Say Never*, author Leo was "a newsreel editor in the New

---

[2]The Encyclopedia of Hollywood, Vol. 3, by Tom & Jim Goldrup

York office of 'News of the Week'. The script is his first produced playwriting effort. Mr. Leo, who has done some radio writing in Hollywood, one time put in a stint as a play reader for Warner Brothers."

The play opened at the Booth Theatre on November 20, 1951. According to its press notes, the play recounted "some fast moving events in the lives of a boy and girl, who are living together without benefit of clergy." At the play's center was Anne Jackson's "Carolie Jones" who was living in Manhattan with one man while an ex-beau tried to win her back. Haim played Maxie Jordan, one of her cosmopolitan neighbors.

Unfortunately, Brooks Atkinson's review in the New York Times damned it with faint praise, offering obligatory kudos to the actors, director, and even the set, but dismissing the play as "a

With Anne Jackson in *Never Say Never* at the Booth Theatre, Haim's first non-musical role on Broadway ("I loved Anne.").

sophomoric piece of sophistication" with nothing of interest to say about young people in post-war America, even for a comedy. As a result, *Never Say Never* closed after only seven performances.

But for H.M., the memory is still a happy one: "I've never not enjoyed being in a play. I never reached a point where I actually criticized the play. I consume it."

Shortly after, Haim's Stage Manager mentor, Karl Nielsen, offered him the Assistant Stage Manager position on *Venus Observed*, billed as "a modern play in blank verse by Christopher Fry" for which Haim would also understudy "Edgar, The Duke's son". The stars were Rex Harrison and Lilli Palmer. The director was Laurence Olivier, who had starred in the play two years earlier in London and had considered taking the lead on Broadway but opted to direct instead, simultaneously starring in the two *Cleopatras* (Shaw's and Shakespeare's) in repertory at New York's Ziegfeld Theatre alongside his wife, Vivian Leigh.

As H.M. recalled, "Rex would have a very tall whisky each night, terrified of the stage. Just terrified. We were all a very congenial family. Everybody liked each other. John Williams was in the play. He was an elegant, wonderful man." Haim toured with the show and ultimately got to play Edgar under Olivier's direction.

"I did get a glimpse into Olivier that few ever saw. We arrived in a new city and I remember getting to the theater before anyone else. I entered from the stage and wandered out into the house, checking out the sight lines. Then I heard Olivier come in. He was up on the stage. He couldn't see me because I was in the dark, so he thought he was alone. He walked right to the lip of the stage, looked out at the audience, and bellowed, 'I'm not afraid of you!' Then he turned around and walked right off."

Venus Observed opened at Haim's old haunt, the New Century, just one day after he turned 25, on February 13, 1952. It completed its scheduled run of 86 performances, closing on April 26.

Shortly after, in May, Ethel Wald became pregnant with Haim's child. It was not planned. Although all secondary sources list their year of marriage as 1951, H.M. revealed they were actually married in 1952. "It was a very simple decision. 'You're pregnant? OK, we'll get married.'" As H.M. elaborated, "We had our ceremony in the basement of a synagogue. There was nobody at the wedding. Just a rabbi, who was a woman. And one other person as a witness. Ethel moved in with me to my one-room apartment."

That winter, Haim found himself working with the same company from *Venus Observed*, again under Stage Manager, Karl Nielsen. Rex Harrison and Lilli Palmer would star once more, with Harrison directing. The play was *The Love of Four Colonels* by playwright-actor Peter Ustinov, a fantasy set around military offi-cers from the four Allied Occupation Powers (American, British, French, and Soviet) of postwar Germany. The London production was a hit and still running after a year-and-a-half, starring Ustinov. Haim was brought on as Assistant Stage Manager for the Broadway premiere and to understudy the role of "Colonel Alexander Ikonen-ko", which he eventually got to play.

"One night, I had to go on very suddenly. It was so sudden that they literally had to push me on stage!" recalled H.M.

It opened at the Shubert Theatre on January 15, 1953. Less than one month later, Haim's first son, William "Billy" Winant, was born on February 11 just one day before Haim's 26th birthday.

"Ethel and I scheduled ourselves in such a way that some-one was always available. I was available during the day while she worked, then I worked at night and Ethel took over."

Haim would head off to the Shubert for *The Love of Four Colonels*, which transferred to the Broadhurst Theatre on April 20 where it closed after a respectable 141 performances on May 16. It was well-received and won "Best Foreign Play" by the New York Drama Critics' Circle.

Less than two months later, on July 5, 1953, Haim would appear on the third season of the live 30-minute TV mystery an-thology series, *The Web*, which had already won two Edgar Awards for its first two seasons and would be nominated the following year for a Primetime Emmy in the now retired category of "Best Mystery, Action or Adventure Program," losing out to *Dragnet*.

It was produced by Mark Goodson and Bill Todman, who would go on to fame and fortune with such classic game shows as *The Price Is Right*, *Family Feud*, *Match Game*, and a host of others. No copies appear to exist of Haim's episode, "A Case of Escape", and the character details are sketchy, but Haim co-starred alongside such notable actors as Ben Gazzara, Raymond Bailey, and Leora Dana. The story involved a man eluding the police who finds out that his own father faced the same situation many years earlier.

Today, H.M. has no recall of this one day of shooting from over seventy years ago, nor does he have instant recall of performing in many of his TV shows, live or taped. As H.M. explained, "It's a job. When you're done, you forget it. It's literally like erasing a blackboard. It's gone! You're not supposed to remember it. If you retained memories of all these things, you'd go crazy. You can't do it. You've got to totally dismiss it. On to the next thing."

To offer another perspective, consider recalling a single workday in one's life from two or three years ago. Now, try seventy years.

Five months later, on December 6, Haim would perform

in another live episode of *The Web*, under the direction of Lela Swift, who would go on to pioneer the groundbreaking gothic soap opera, *Dark Shadows*, but this time, Haim would shoot in the day and then rush to the Martin Beck Theatre at night to perform in not only his biggest Broadway success, but the one that would lead him to Hollywood — playing "Mr. Seiko" in the original Broadway cast of *The Teahouse of the August Moon*, one of the very few plays to win Broadway's triple crown: Best Play from both the Tony Awards and New York Drama Critics Circle, and the Pulitzer Prize for Drama.

BALANCING BROADWAY AND LIVE TELEVISION (1954-1956)

The hottest show on Broadway... and the call from Hollywood.

"Theater is something I can touch. It's mine. Film is not.
It's got a beginning, a middle and an end, every night.

The Teahouse of the August Moon opened at Broadway's Martin Beck Theatre on October 15, 1953. Set in a rural Japanese village in 1946 amidst the temporary, post-war, American occupation, it was ahead of its time in calling out American arrogance and cultural ignorance by disguising its critiques under the cozy trappings of light comedy.

The fusion of entertainment and ideas worked like a charm with both audiences and critics (not to mention the Pulitzer Prize committee), bringing about high praise from Brooks Atkinson in the New York Times, whose words may have caused Haim's *Never Say Never* to close after only seven performances, but with *Teahouse*, helped propell the play to run for 2½ years and 1,027 performances.

At the center of the play was Sakini, the hired interpreter between local Japanese villagers and the condescending American officers. This allows Sakini to speak in broken English to the

American characters (and directly to the audience) while speaking in Japanese to his fellow villagers. One can only assume that having characters speak in Japanese, with no translation, was a bit revelatory for Broadway audiences in 1953.

Just as Sakini was played in a unanimously celebrated performance by Caucasian actor, David Wayne, so too, did Haim take on the role of Mr. Seiko, one of the Japanese villagers who would find himself assigned by Sakini as the new Chief of Agriculture in

As Mr. Seiko in the original Broadway cast
of *Teahouse of the August Moon.*

the village. Like most of the villagers, Haim spoke only Japanese in the play, which was written out for the actors phonetically, just as it is in the published version of the play. A few years earlier, Wayne had won the Tony Award for Best Actor in a Musical for *Finian's Rainbow*. For *Teahouse*, he would win Best Actor for Drama.

"David Wayne was always concerned about everyone," H.M. remembered. "It was his company. With the star of the show, it's always his company or her company. A good star who wants to get the most out of it isn't aloof. He gets involved in everyone's problems. And David did that."

Conversely, H.M. recalled of John Forsythe, who had the non-Japanese lead role of American Captain Fisby, "John Forsythe was more elegant, more to himself. You couldn't really be buddy-buddy with him. He was on *his* level.".

Given the length of the run, Wayne ultimately moved on, being replaced by notable actors both on Broadway and on tour. H.M. was most impressed by Burgess Meredith when he assumed the role of Sakini: "Burgess Meredith *was* Sakini.".

As for Eli Wallach as Sakini: "It was like a Jew playing the part," recalled H.M. with amusement. "It was all wrong. But he was wonderful. A great actor, but wrong casting."

When it closed on March 24, 1956, *Teahouse* was the 11th

longest running play in Broadway history, behind only *The Seven Year Itch*. But today, despite its critical and financial success, its Tony and Pulitzer, it is largely remembered for the 1956 movie version and its controversial casting of Marlon Brando in "yellow face" as Sakini. Many who criticize or dismiss *Teahouse* have never actually seen nor read the play, let alone watched the movie. The butt of the jokes in the movie is the Americans, never the Japanese. Still, one can only imagine the different place in history the play and film adaptation might hold if a Japanese actor had been cast as Sakini. All other Japanese roles, including Haim's role of Seiko, were re-cast with Asian actors in the film version. But like something akin to a woman always being cast as Peter in James Barrie's *Peter Pan*, *Teahouse* seemed dead-set on casting a Caucasian as Sakini, further exacerbated on the big Cinemascope screen (despite William Tuttle's exceptional make-up for Brando).

From the original Broadway cast, only Paul Ford as the brilliantly buffoonish Colonel Wainright III was cast in the movie version, but even then, only because the actor originally cast in the film, Louis Calhern (Oscar nominated in 1950's *The Magnificent Yankee*), had died suddenly after arriving in Japan for the shoot. Since the actor who replaced Calhern would have no time to prepare, who better than Ford, who had played the role over 1000 times. In the years since, the few revivals of the play have cast only Asians in the Japanese roles, including Sakini, but regardless, to date, the play has never been performed again on Broadway.

For Haim, the new cache of performing nightly in a hit Broadway show translated into being cast over and over in the daytime during that same period in the escalating boom-town of New York's live television scene. 1955 became a particularly busy year for Haim, perfectly demonstrating the unique life of a work-ing actor juggling stage at night with TV during the day.

First up was an early live daily soap opera called *Modern Romances*, hosted by Martha Scott. Haim performed for five days straight, from Monday, January 24, 1955 through Friday, January 28 in the five, 15-minute episode storyline titled, "The Nice Young Man", appearing with Lee Remick and Steven Hill. Copies do not exist, but Internet Movie Database (IMDB) describes the storyline thusly: "This five part episode narrates the story of a nice young man who initially is the victim of a frame-up, but swiftly starts to realize that in reality, he very much likes the beautiful girls who are responsible for the framing, with predictable results."

On May 1 of '55, Haim would appear on-screen for the first of what would be many times with a movie legend from his child-hood. This time, with Boris Karloff in the *General Electric The-ater* presentation of the offbeat, surreal "Mr. Blue Ocean". Karloff played the title role, a lonely widower, abandoned by his sons, who begins to court "Rain Drop" (Susan Strasberg), but soon finds himself challenged for her affections by "West Wind" (Anthony Perkins) and "Earth Quake" (Haim). H.M. remembered Karloff as being "a true gentleman," but little else about the production as he was bouncing from one TV show to the next, thinking of them as disposable jobs, not historic memories to hold on to. Haim does remember that twelve days later, on May 13, Ethel would give birth to their second child, Scott.

A month later, on June 12, Haim would appear live with Carlos Montalban (Ricardo's father) in an episode of the Revlon-sponsored anthology series, *Appointment With Danger*, titled "The Secret of Juan Valdez". This was Haim's first professional interaction with the Montalban family (he would work closely with Ricardo multiple times). "Over the years, I got very close with the Montalbans," H.M. recalled with a smile. "We were like family.".

On September 10, Haim appeared on the Dupont Television Network with Jack Carson in the *Studio 57* presentation of "Who's Been Sitting in My Car?". The Dupont network would only exist one more year, resulting in the remaining big three networks that would vie for power for decades: CBS, ABC, NBC. For that show, H.M. remembered, "I did a scene live, thought I was done. I started to change, walked off the set. They got me and literally threw me onto the set. I came into the scene going through a wall!".

The next month, Haim would appear un-billed and shirt-less in his first non-live TV show, *The Phil Silvers Show*, with the comedian starring as his iconic conman and master manipulator, Sgt. Bilko. Haim's episode, "The Boxer", was the sixth episode of the very first season, airing on October 25, 1955. "It was shot with three cameras, on film, but no audience. It was one day and I was in and out." recalled H.M. It would reunite him with his *Teahouse* costar, Paul Ford, undoubtedly cast as Bilko's long-suffering Col-onel Hall because of his similarly blustery turn in *Teahouse*.

Haim would do a few more live anthology TV shows back-to-back, but his biggest career event of 1956 didn't happen on stage, screen, nor television. It happened at New York's Plaza Ho-tel.

Hollywood agent, Henry Wilson had sent Haim a mes-sage through David Wayne that he would like to meet. Wilson had played a large role in developing "the beefcake craze" of the 1950s. He was known for his stable of young, hunky male clients, nearly all of whom he personally rechristened with hyperbolically macho Anglo names, including Rock Hudson (Roy Scherer, Jr.), Tab Hunter (Arthur Kelm), Chad Everett (Ramon Cramton), Guy Madison (Robert Moseley), Troy Donahue (Merle Johnson, Jr.), Rory Calhoun (Francis McCown), and John Saxon (Carmine Orri-co). He wisely left Robert Wagner's name alone.

"He named everybody! Who would think of a name like Guy Madison?!"

As H.M. continued, "We met at the Plaza Hotel and he said he would like to represent me, and I said, 'Terrific.' He asked, 'When are you coming to Hollywood?' I told him, 'Never. I'm not coming to Hollywood. I'm a stage actor.' But then I said, 'If you have something for me, let me know.' Well, toward the end of the run of *Teahouse*, Wilson called, saying he got me a really nice role in a western for RKO that Sam Fuller was producing, writing, and directing."

That film was *Run of the Arrow*, to star recent Academy Award winner, Rod Steiger.

Chapter Five

HOLLYWOOD BIG SCREEN DEBUT (1956)

Playing Indian with Charles Bronson, Rod Steiger, and Sam Fuller.

*"I never saw myself in film.
I never wanted to be a movie star, just a working actor."*

"I took the plane to Los Angeles. Coach was in the front, the first six seats. As you board, they gave you a little sack with a sandwich, carton of milk, and an apple. The back part of the plane had sleepers. Up and down, two beds. This was before the jet engine. Remember, these were 11-hour trips from New York to Los Angeles in a propeller plane!"

Haim was picked up at the airport by his new agent, who was already notorious for sleeping with his young male discoveries upon arrival.

"I knew all about Henry's reputation. We went to his house, up in

First Hollywood headshot.

the hills off Sunset Boulevard. I was given an alcove with a bed. He made one slight pass at me. One. I said no and he never bothered me again. I was his 'New York actor'; that's what he called me to excuse the fact that he wasn't having sex with me."

Wilson found Haim a studio apartment on Fuller, south of Sunset. "There was a Ralph's Market right on the corner, which is still there today."

There were a few months of downtime for Haim to prep for his role in *Run of the Arrow*, including horseback-riding and bow-and-arrow instruction. Haim, however, surprised the studio by being more proficient than they had imagined. In his native Detroit, Haim had gone out to the country with school friends and rode horses, taking to them right away.

"I always had a special connection with horses, and especially with the horses assigned to me for the

As Crazy Wolf with Rod Steiger in Sam Fuller's *Run of the Arrow*. Note the indigenous actors behind Steiger and H.M.

duration of films I worked on," H.M. related with fondness. "I was always very sad to part with them when the film was over. Always."

Haim's role would be that of Crazy Wolf, a war hungry, white-hating Sioux warrior under the more peaceful chief, Blue Buffalo (Charles Bronson). Fuller's script paralleled these two Sioux with their white military counterparts: Brian Keith's calm and thoughtful Captain Clark and his Indian-hating, war hungry Lieutenant Driscoll (Ralph Meeker).

If casting Haim as an Indian in his first Hollywood movie seemed like an odd choice, it was actually not only standard for Hollywood, but for Wilson in particular. In 1950, one of the very first major speaking roles Wilson had procured for his new find,

On horseback alongside Charles Bronson as the chief, Blue Buffalo, in *Run of the Arrow*.

Rock Hudson, was as Young Bull, an Indian warrior, in Anthony Mann's *Winchester '73*. Just like Hudson, Haim would also be shirtless for the entire film, but fortunately, he would not have to wear the false nose that Hudson was given.

Prior to going on location to shoot the film, Wilson wisely got Haim into some TV shows so he could get familiar with the workings of a Hollywood set. First up was a day at Republic Studios in North Hollywood for a second season episode of *Alfred Hitchcock Presents* called "De Mortuis". Haim had a key, one-scene bit as a truck driver described by others as "good looking", who successfully hits on the lead's cheating wife.

This was followed by a second season episode of *Gunsmoke*

H.M.'s very first appearance on the big screen in Hollywood, surprising Jay C. Flippen and Rod Steiger in *Run of the Arrow*.

called, "Spring Term". It was a minor role, but the first of his eight *Gunsmoke* episodes over the next sixteen years.

Finally, on March 6 of '56, Haim appeared in an episode of the long-running daily live TV show, *Matinee Theater*, "The Book of Ruth", starring Sarah Churchill.

When he wasn't working or training, 29-year-old Haim explored Hollywood's social scene: "We always went swimming at the Beverly Hills Hotel. I had friends who lived there. One day, I saw Natalie Wood was on the diving board, she was getting ready to dive in, and I jumped up and screamed 'Wait!' She was wearing a huge bracelet on her left wrist and I wanted to let her know. She heard me, smiled, and waved me off. I finally found out the next day that she wore the bracelet to cover up a deformity on her wrist."

Prior to the start of principal photography on *Run of the Arrow*, Wilson discussed with Sam Fuller changing Haim's name (he had been billed as Haim Winant in his recent Los Angeles TV shows). The last name was too easy to mispronounce. The correct pronunciation is "Why-Nant" but people would often say "Win-Ant" as in "winning". It was agreed that the spelling would be changed from Winant to "Wynant". But what to do with "Haim"? After much volleying of ideas, someone (It may have been Fuller, but H.M. isn't positive) arrived at "H.M."

"*He Man* is how Henry Wilson sold it to me."

Run of the Arrow started shooting on location in Arizona and Saint George, Utah, on June 19, 1956. "I met Sam Fuller for the first time on set. He'd shoot a real gun to call action and shoot it again to call cut. One time on location, I sat in on dailies. Sam's wife was in the room and was openly admiring me up on the screen, shirtless. I was in the best shape of my life. Well, I don't think Sam liked that because the next day we did the scene where an arrow is shot and I take off barefoot in the direction of the arrow, running into the distance. Bang! Action! I ran at top speed. I kept running and running, waiting for the second gunshot for 'Cut!' but it never came. Finally, I was so exhausted that I stopped running. Well, the joke was on me because the entire crew had already broken for lunch!".

Despite this, H.M.'s memories of Fuller are warm and positive: "He was a brilliant man, always in charge. This movie was way ahead of its time. He not only wrote and directed, but produced! This was a Sam Fuller set."

In Fuller's progressive scenario (which seems to have had a heavy influence on 1990's *Dances With Wolves*), Rod Steiger plays O'Meara, an angry Johnny Reb who loves his country but will not accept joining the post-Civil War United States. O'Meara heads west to find himself and in the process finds the Sioux who, after first trying to kill him, adopt him as one of their own, which puts him in conflict with the US cavalry.

H.M. remembered, "The word that comes to mind for Rod Steiger is 'dominant'. Whenever he was on set, it was all about him. But I did like him. Sarita Montiel had an issue with him. He was full of pimples and sores, so to have this man lean all over you was not easy for her. Sarita had a heavy accent, so they knew they were going to dub her from Day One. That's Angie Dickinson's voice in the movie. But Sarita looked and acted the role perfectly."

"I liked Brian Keith. I can just see him in one scene, in his uniform, with the top off, in his underwear, and he's playing with his guns. I remember that moment. He was totally relaxed and I

Vengeful Doppelgängers, Crazy Wolf (H.M.) and Lt. Driscoll (Ralph Meeker), with the latter getting his just reward in *Run of the Arrow*.

admired that in him as an actor."

"Jay C. Flippen was a wonderful old guy except he wasn't that old. He was in his late fifties, but he looked so old to me!"

"Charlie Bronson and I thought we were two Hollywood studs. We'd go cruise the town. We'd totally strike out. Zero! They couldn't care less about us."

"I also became buddies with Ralph Meeker for a little while. We spent time at the Garden of Allah in West Hollywood. We were both bad guys in the movie, but he was badder. Crazy Wolf was honorable, but Ralph's character was really bad. I had a code and he didn't."

"The only thing I didn't enjoy about making *Run of the Arrow* is that it was very cold and every morning, they sprayed me with equally cold full body makeup to darken my skin. It was freezing in the morning, then hot in the afternoon."

H.M. initiating the title challenge in *Run of the Arrow*.

Just as he did when playing a dancing extra in *So Young, So Bad* five years earlier, H.M. takes the big screen by storm. His Crazy Wolf is dynamic, impassioned, principled, and possessed of unexpected glimmers of humor. But make no mistake, he *will* kill you. There was no doubt that H.M. Wynant could hold his own on movie screens with a cast of Hollywood heavy hitters.

When the production wrapped, the newly re-branded "H.M. Wynant" was feeling positive about his relocated life: "The money was good, the future looked very bright. I brought Ethel and the boys out here. While I was shooting in Saint George, Utah, they came to Los Angeles and set up in a beautiful Spanish house in the valley that Henry Wilson found for us.".

"New York was finished for me."

Chapter Six

HOLLYWOOD SMALL SCREEN DEBUT (1956-1957)

Playhouse 90 with Mickey Rooney, Errol Flynn,
and Jack Palance

"Once they establish you as an Indian, they say 'Get that Indian!'
They don't even know your name!"

After *Run of the Arrow* wrapped shooting at the end of Summer, 1956, it would not be released until Fall, 1957. Agent Henry Wilson was patient, willing to wait for good roles to build the careers of his hunky movie star discoveries. H.M., however, just wanted to work:

"Henry Wilson was against me doing TV. We had a big argument about it. He said if you really want to be a movie star, do not do Television. He was only interested in me as a movie star. I said, fine, that's wonderful, but while I'm waiting around to be a movie star, I want to work! So, he kept after the movie roles and brought on someone else to help get me TV work, because that was not his interest at all."

Some of H.M.'s most impressive work was done during this period for the classic CBS anthology series, *Playhouse 90*. From 1956 to 1960, it produced 133 90-minute episodes, most of them live, featuring the work of some of our finest film actors, many at the start of their careers, some at the end. It featured original teleplays by the likes of Rod Serling, Horton Foote, and Abby Mann, and launched the careers of young movie directors like John Frankenheimer, Arthur Penn, and George Roy Hill, to name just a few. It would go on to win thirteen Emmy Awards, two Golden Globes, and two Peabody Awards.

The first of H.M.'s six episodes was one of the rare, non-live, filmed episodes, "Massacre at Sand Creek" from the first season. Airing on December 27, 1956, it was written and produced by William Sackheim (*First Blood*) and directed by Arthur Hiller (*Love Story*, *The Americanization of Emily*, *The In-Laws*). Just as Sam Fuller had done with *Run of the Arrow*, the producers of *Playhouse 90* boldly told a story that dispelled the Western myth of the "Noble American Soldier" vs the "Indian Savage". The events, though fictionalized, were based on a shameful piece of American history wherein U.S. soldiers made a peace treaty with the Cheyenne in 1864 only to betray and massacre them as they slept, killing hundreds, including women and children.

H.M. was again cast as an Indian, Free Horse, a Cheyenne brave who in the opening was indebted to star John Derek's Lt. Norman Tucker. With H.M. channeling both the character's integrity and ferocity, it is Free Horse who frames the story, survives the brutal massacre orchestrated by Colonel John Templeton (Everett Sloane, staple of Orson Welles' Mercury Theatre), and carries out Tucker's dying wish: to bring the evidence of the tragedy to Washington so that Templeton can be punished. Rounding out the outstanding cast were Gene Evans and William Schallert.

Despite continuing the policy of casting white actors in the major Indian roles, the episode utilized a Blackfoot Indian, Steve Drumm, as the make-up and hair expert to ensure authenticity.

Recalled H.M., "Arthur Hiller only commented if there was something amiss. It's a good way to direct. He created the atmosphere so you can do good work. Give the actor the first chance. If they're any decent actor, they know what to do."

H.M. followed this with another Season One episode: the classic, "The Comedian", which was broadcast live on Valentine's Day, 1957, with an Emmy-winning script (from a story by Ernest Lehman) by Rod Serling, hot off his Emmy-winning teleplay earlier that season for *Requiem for a Heavyweight*, and direction by John Frankenheimer (*The Manchurian Candidate*, *Seven Days in May*). At a time when powerhouse comedians like Sid Caesar and Milton Berle (on whom the title character was rumored to be based) were ruling the airwaves, it told the uncompromisingly vicious story of megalomaniacal TV star Sammy Hogarth (Mickey Rooney, who received a well-deserved Emmy nomination for his jaw-droppingly nasty performance) who was cruel and abusive to everyone he came in contact with, including his meek brother/ whipping-boy, played affectingly by singer Mel Tormé, and his long-suffering head writer, played by Edmund O'Brien, who had two affable writers on his staff, one of whom is "Sonny", played by H.M.

"Mickey Rooney would show up to rehearsals with another beautiful woman every day. 'Is there a place for her?' he'd ask Frankenheimer. And there would be. Over the years, I got close with Frankenheimer through my wife, Ethel, who worked with Johnny regularly over the decades. He and I were dart fanatics. We'd play at a pub. He had a board at his house, but it was poorly mounted. On set, Frankenheimer (then 27) was childlike. He was one of us and yet not quite. He was treated like a kid and acted like a wonderful young man. He was not old enough to be mean yet." H.M. would have turned 30 just two days before it aired live.

"Working on *Playhouse 90* always started with a table read," remembered H.M. "A long, long, long table. Everybody there, including crew and all actors, even if you only had one line. We'd read the script as if we were doing the show. But you never get up from your chair. Then, the director would break it up into pieces that would be staged and rehearsed. The sets were already built when we showed up. By the time we got up from the table, we knew so much (about) who we were and what we were doing that it didn't need 'staging', we just knew where to go, who to look at, where to sit, to stand — it became natural."

Sonny was a fun, if undemanding, little role for H.M. in a powerhouse production that won the Emmy for "Outstanding Single Program of the Year", but H.M.'s personal best work for *Playhouse 90* was still to come.

The next month, H.M. found himself in Tucson, Arizona to shoot another filmed *Playhouse 90*: "Without Incident", an effective western potboiler starring Errol Flynn, who was 47 at the time of production, but looked much worse for the wear, following years of drinking, smoking, and narcotics abuse. As H.M. recalled:

"On my first day on set, I kept looking for Errol Flynn, who was a hero of mine. I didn't see him, but I did see an old man

As a disgraced soldier, commanded by Errol Flynn, in the filmed *Playhouse 90* episode, "Without Incident".

slumped in a chair. They lit and staged the scene with stand-ins and then they called Mr. Flynn to set. Suddenly the old guy put one boot on, then the other boot on, practically crawled towards where his mark was, but with every step he got younger, every step he lost five years. By the time he hit his mark, he was Errol Flynn!"

Flynn's Captain Bidlack had been assigned to protect no-nonsense older sister, Kathy (Ann Sheridan) and her flirty younger sister, Angela (Julie London), and bring to justice the Apache who had murdered their respective husbands.

"I was in awe of the two ladies in this, even then - Ann Sheridan and Julie London. They needed us as much as we needed them. We all gave to each other. It became a very good unit. Everything came out perfectly right."

The 90-minute episode featured H.M.'s most significant and demanding TV role yet, that of a disgraced member of Flynn's unit who had been a deserter at Gettysburg and whose punishment was having his head shorn.

"I remember the bald cap! I couldn't shave my head because Wilson had booked me immediately after in *Decision at Sundown* at Columbia where I needed my hair. They made a skin wig for me and it was very good. In those days they accommodated me. Boy, are those days gone!"

H.M. played a volatile loner. A simpleton who was thought

a coward, he overcompensated by constantly declaring his fearlessness. Like many casualties of war, the tragedy of his character was simply that he was emotionally and intellectually ill-equipped to handle the rigors of battle. As a result, he and London's Angela find a sort of "outsider kinship" and share several very affecting scenes. His character's desperation would ultimately cost him his life. Airing on June 6, 1957, it was conceived and directed by Charles Marquis Warren, a prolific western writer who would go on to create TV's *Rawhide* and *The Virginian* (H.M. would guest star in both).

After "Without Incident", Wilson had H.M. scheduled at Columbia for *Decision at Sundown* (1957), the third of six highly

With Julie London, playing a fellow outcast in the group, in *Playhouse 90's* "Without Incident". H.M. wore a skullcap because he needed a full head of hair on Budd Boetticher's *Decision at Sundown*, opposite Randolph Scott.

regarded collaborations between director Budd Boetticher and actor Randolph Scott between 1956 and 1960. All but two were written by Burt Kennedy, *Decision at Sundown* being one of the two written by Charles Lang. A seventh Boetticher/Scott film, *Westbound* (1958), was done quickly, to fulfill a contractual obligation Scott had over at Warners, and is largely considered not on par with the others. Often referred to as the "Ranown Westerns" (the films were a producing partnership between Scott and Harry Joe Brown), the movies were finely detailed, yet fast-moving chamber-dramas-on-the-range that seemed to effortlessly convey basic truths about human nature, violence, love, and manhood.

Sergio Leone admitted to being highly influenced by the Ranown westerns in developing Clint Eastwood's "Man with No Name" character. However, *Decision at Sundown* breaks with that model in showing Scott's character as atypically flawed and driven by revenge in tribute to his dead wife, who he learns was far from the saint he believes her to be. It is also unlike the others in that it is locked into interiors, as opposed to the outdoor journeys and striking vistas of the other films.

Shot close to Los Angeles, in Agoura, California, for six weeks, beginning April 15, 1957, H.M. played the deputy, referred to as "Spanish". With a jet-black dye job and heavy, tan makeup, it is unclear if "Spanish" is the character's given name or a nickname to suggest some form of Latin ethnicity. Spanish and his boss, the Sheriff (Andrew Duggan) are in the pocket of rich, corrupt, town czar, Tate Kimbrough (John Carroll), for whom Scott has come gunning, accompanied by his sidekick, Sam (the ever affable Noah Beery, Jr.). Like many of H.M.'s early film roles, it is a very physical performance, with him seemingly doing his own stunts.

As H.M. recalled, "I remember having the gun out and sneaking low across the street and under the windows so I couldn't be seen by Randy Scott." And then he added with a laugh, "And that's all I remember!" Moments later, Spanish tries to shoot Scott but gets his arm impaled on a hay bale hook wielded by Sam. Later, to prove his worth to Kimbrough, Spanish shoots Sam in the back, immediately getting fatal return fire from Scott.

Despite his now-vague memories of making the movie, H.M. recalled, "Budd was a very good director. And Karen Steele! Such a beauty. Everybody on set tried to hump her. Everybody!" What the cast didn't know at the time was that Steele and Budd were having their own extramarital affair, which resulted in a brief engagement after Budd separated from his wife. The two, however, never wed.

While H.M. was shooting *Decision at Sundown*, Wilson sent a short blurb out that was picked up by the North American Newspaper Alliance, running in many papers nationwide:

TV-Movie Actor Uses Initials

Hollywood, Cal. — A young stage and television character actor has joined the small, select ranks of players who use two initials instead of first names for screen credits. He is H.M. Wynant, born Chiam (sic) Winant in Detroit 30 years ago.

Coming here nine months ago from a Broadway and New York television career in which he was credited as Hiam (sic) Winant, the actor had his name changed by a Hollywood agent to H.M. Wynant and as such is doing nicely in both movies and TV.

— The Evening Sun, Baltimore, Maryland (4/25/57)

Another significant announcement that occurred in the first week of the April shoot was that Ethel gave birth to their third and final child, Bruce, born at St. John's Hospital in Santa Monica on April 9. H.M. and Ethel now had the financial responsibility of a four-year-old, a three-year-old, and a newborn, so H.M.'s preference to move from one job to the next, with no downtime, was in full bloom.

With *Decision at Sundown* shooting just outside of Los Angeles and his next film not starting until July 29th in Bend, Oregon, H.M.'s Spring and early Summer were jam-packed with TV work on episodes of *Wire Service, Lux Video Theatre, Climax!,* and *Navy Log*, all of which allowed him to spend time in Los Angeles with his growing family.

Regarding the importance of having family as the foundation of his career, H.M. remarked, "A wheel has a center, you've got to have that center or you have no wheel."

Oregon Passage was shot in Deschutes National Forest, just outside of Bend, Oregon, for Allied Artists in the Summer of 1957. H.M. remembered, "Bend, Oregon, was the smallest of the small towns. A tiny little town with a big field outside where people shoot. The town was maybe two houses and one store. They did have two strings of 2-story cabins. That's where the cast and crew was put up."

It was H.M.'s first widescreen, Cinemascope film and also the first film which featured him prominently in the poster art. H.M.'s Shoshone warrior, Black Eagle, was the heart of the film's danger and its advertising campaign. And yet here, as with *Run of the Arrow*, H.M.'s name is not in the poster credit block. H.M. theorized, "It was almost as if you were discriminated against for *playing* an Indian. All the white leads would get credited on the poster, but if you played an Indian, even if your part was just as big - or bigger! - you wouldn't get the same consideration."

For his role, H.M. spoke no English. At first listen, one would instantly believe that H.M. had been taught Shoshone or had his lines written phonetically (as with his spoken Japanese in *Teahouse of the August Moon*), but such was not the case for films on such tight budgets and schedules. As H.M. recalled:

"I was expected to make it up. And I did! But I took it very seriously. When I spoke, it was consistent because I know what I'm doing and therefore what I'm *saying*."

H.M. enjoyed the production and his large role, climaxing with a magnificent, brutal fight between him and star, John Ericson, but H.M. also recalls that there was a lot of off-screen pining for the attention of female lead, Lola Albright.

"There was myself, a stunt guy, and Lola Albright. And we were all in her room, the three of us. And the stunt guy and I were waiting each other out, seeing who was going to leave. It must have been an hour. Finally, I left. I couldn't handle it anymore. I took off. 'You can have her!'"

According to H.M., around this time, he was offered the role of "Mike Hammer" in the new TV series of the same name, based on the Mickey Spillane detective character, but he turned it down. It ultimately went to Darren McGavin. "The idea seemed repulsive to me to play one role. As I said, my agent didn't want me to do TV at all, so it was an easy decision to say no. I enjoyed working in TV, but the fun was playing different characters all the time, on different shows."

September 5, 1957 was a double-header for H.M. — not only was *Run of the Arrow* released, but it was also the night in which he performed in his fourth *Playhouse 90*, the Second Season opener after its multi-Emmy Award winning First Season, once again directed by John Frankenheimer. The episode was "The Death of Manolete", performed live, and starred Jack Palance, who had just won the Best Actor Emmy for the previous season's "Requiem for a Heavyweight", which had won a total of five Emmys.

"I liked Jack. We got along great. Everybody was afraid of him because he had a look that was scary. He was a nice man, but you wouldn't think that to look at him. You'd back off."

In this 90-minute look at the life of one of Spain's most celebrated bullfighters (Palance), H.M. played Marquez, a rival bullfighter who is ultimately gored in the arena. Remembered H.M., "I had to do a lot of cape work. I remember rehearsing in my room, over and over, until I got really good at it."

On another costar, character actor Robert Middleton, H.M. distinctly recalled, "Robert Middleton always carried a pocketful of money. Always hundreds of dollars in his pockets. He was a poker player, a total fanatic. So anywhere he could get a game, he would. Even on set."

Immediately after, H.M. found himself working on the biggest film yet of his career. A genuine "A-Picture" starring two of the biggest movie stars Hollywood ever produced.

Chapter Seven

BIG FINISH TO THE 1950's

Clark Gable, Burt Lancaster, Ricardo Montalban,
George C. Scott … and a Disney scandal.

*"I was 'The New York Actor', so out of 50 people,
they'd pick me. I was constantly working."*

Eleven days after "The Death of Manolete", H.M. was at the Samuel Goldwyn Studios in Hollywood opposite Clark Gable and Burt Lancaster for the Hecht-Hill-Lancaster production of *Run Silent, Run Deep* (1958), It was the first feature screenplay by celebrated anthology TV writer, John Gay, from the novel by Commander Edward L. Beach, directed by Robert Wise (*West Side Story, The Sound of Music*), and released through United Artists.

Gable plays the captain of a submarine that had been sunk by the Japanese during World War 2. He is now a commander in charge of a new sub and crew where there is question from his lieutenant (Lancaster) as to whether the motivation for Gable's perilous choices might be revenge.

"They built an entire submarine on a soundstage - to scale! It truly felt like we were all on a real submarine."

Oddly, the movie has no tail credits, so while H.M.'s role of Hendrix, the crew medic, was significant, he and many other mem-

As medic, Hendrix, tending to a dying Clark Gable while Jack Warden stands by in *Run Silent, Run Deep*. Soon after, H.M. and Warden would share TV's first on-screen male-to-male "kiss" - live no less!

bers of the cast were not credited on the film itself, which was a strange and unfortunate oversight. Regardless, H.M. remembered:

"Everybody was a good, working team. Everybody was equal, we were all actors. Period. Lancaster was the producer, but didn't act like a boss. He was an actor on that set. There were discussions, but nothing of a harsh nature. Wise ran the set so well you didn't know he was there. Extremely professional."

Don Rickles, in his big screen debut in a dramatic role, was one of the few crewmen who received on-screen credit. "I never saw a more nervous, sweaty actor in my life. But he was wonderful!"

H.M. is part of the ensemble throughout the film, but the highlight was working with his idol, Clark Gable, in his one-on-one scene after Gable's character takes ill. Seeing a youthful H.M.'s similarly masculine features and energy opposite Gable's faded good looks added an extra layer to a powerful scene wherein H.M. confidentially explained to Gable the gravity of his condition.

"It was a lovely little scene. Gable was God and I had his head in my hand." H.M. further recalled, "At that time, Gable had palsy. At 5pm, a nurse would come and he'd be gone. They tried to shoot around his condition, but you can see him shaking in some scenes."

Working on *Run Silent, Run Deep* gave H.M. a big boost of cache. As a result, the remainder of 1957 and the start of 1958 led to back-to-back episodes of *M Squad, Cheyenne, Zorro, Broken Arrow, Mackenzie's Raiders,* and the first of two guest roles on *Mike Hammer* (a series lead he had turned down). He also appeared in his first episode of *Perry Mason,* in which he would appear a total of ten times over the show's nine seasons.

However, at the start of May, H.M. returned to CBS for his fifth episode of *Playhouse 90* titled, "Nightmare at Ground Zero", broadcast live on May 15, 1958. Written by Paul Monash (*Peyton*

Place, *Salem's Lot*) and directed by Franklin Schaffner (*Patton*, *Planet of the Apes*), H.M. played one of a five-scientist firing party, stationed in a bunker 20 miles from the disastrous 1954 hydrogen bomb test that took place on Bikini Atoll in the Marshall Islands. H.M., the laid-back cut-up of the group, is introduced smoking a cigarette and wearing a Hawaiian shirt as the docu-drama voice-over informs us he is "David Green, handling certain optical and electronic experiments". Things do not fare well for the five men as the effects of the blast were seriously underestimated. Jack Warden is one of the other five members, led by Barry Sullivan.

"Jack Warden and I did the first male-to-male kiss on TV! I was drowning in about four inches of water and Jack was giving me mouth-to-mouth. On live television!"

Recreating a nuclear catastrophe on live TV is not without its own potential for hazard, as H.M. recalled, "During one of the explosions, a metal locker was designed to fall on me. It wound up crushing my finger. It's still deformed to this day."

"Years later, I remember going to Franklin Schaffner's house and he had his Oscar on the mantle. I went over to it, picked it up, and realized it was covered with dust. It was filthy!"

Two weeks later, H.M. was in Oregon, working for the first time with Walt Disney Productions on the feature film, *Tonka*, starring 19-year-old Sal Mineo as the 16-year-old brave-in-training, White Bull, who, in his failed attempt to capture a wild horse, defies his cocky and cruel warrior cousin, Yellow Bull (H.M.), losing his cousin's prized rope in the process. White Bull makes amends by capturing the colt (which he dubs "Tonka" for "Great One") and returns Yellow Bull's rope. But for Yellow

H.M. (left) as Sal Mineo's cruel, older cousin, Yellow Bull, in Disney's *Tonka*.

Bull, this is not enough — he wants Tonka, too. The matter is brought to Chief Sitting Bull (John War Eagle), who explains that rank has its privileges. Tonka now belongs to Yellow Bull, who proceeds to beat the colt into submission. White Bull cannot stand the cruelty of his cousin, so he sets Tonka free. After the horse is briefly captured by a group of horse traders (led by Slim Pickens), he is sold to the kindly Captain Keogh (Philip Carey), who names him "Comanche".

One of two striking studio portraits taken for Disney's *Tonka*.

All of this horse trade culminates in the arrival of the arrogant, Indian-hating General George Armstrong Custer (Britt Lomond) into Keogh's camp, insisting there is no such thing as a peaceful Indian and plotting to raid Sitting Bull's Sioux tribe at the Little Big Horn. Well, we all know how that turned out. As the opening credits inform us, this movie is the story of the one cavalry survivor of the Little Big Horn: Tonka.

In terms of H.M.'s charismatic and brutal Yellow Bull, he proves his worth as a warrior, killing many cavalrymen, including Keogh. At one point, it looks like both Tonka and White Bull have also died in battle, leading the viewer to question whether this is actually the Walt Disney family film they had bought a ticket for. But within moments, almost Christ-like, both White Bull and Tonka rise from seemingly certain-death, the latter recognizing Yellow

Bull and trampling his tormentor to death.

A large portion of the colorfully shot *Tonka* takes place between a teenage boy and his horse as they play together and train together, scene after scene. This is clearly a movie for young boys and girls who love horses. In terms

Wider view of H.M. for second *Tonka* studio portrait.

of H.M.'s sub-filmography playing an Indian, it is the first time he is not required to go bare-chested for any part of the film, although Mineo does those honors for his teen fans.

H.M. recalled that Mineo was a nice young fellow, but hardly the naive young boy he often portrayed, "There was a poker game in Mineo's suite every night!"

H.M. relayed a particularly graphic memory of character actor, Slim Pickens: "He played the main wrangler. He had one stunt he was doing on a horse. He fell off the horse and went right into the tree and broke his nose. To my eyes, his nose was lying right on his cheek. Slim got up, straightened it out with his hands, and said 'That's okay, it probably looks better,' and he went right on working!"

The film was a hit for Disney and put H.M. in good stead with the studio, so much so that he was immediately cast as a villainous series regular in episodes 5 and 6 of "Texas John Slaughter", which was in the first of its three seasons for *The Magical World of Disney* on ABC, starring Tom Tryon as an adventurous, historically-based Texas Ranger. H.M. was cast as Yancy, one of Slaughter's crew, who made no secret of his animosity towards Slaughter, nor that he'd put a bullet in him, given the chance. Despite various guest villains appearing in weekly episodes, it was clear that Yancy was intended to be a series regular antagonist. But after two episodes, Yancy (and H.M.) mysteriously vanished with no on-screen explanation. But there was an off-screen reason:

"I got fired on a morals clause in my contract due to an affair I'd had in Oregon when I was doing *Tonka*. The woman turned out to be the girlfriend of someone very important at the studio. Fortunately, Disney wanted to bury it, so it worked to my advantage. I'm very lucky to have survived that. I finished what I had to do on *Slaughter* and then it was bye-bye from Disney forever. You don't do that. I was stupid."

H.M. can't be positive, but it may have also led to the end

of his relationship with his agent, Henry Wilson. The scandal, coupled with H.M. continuing to say yes to any TV guest role that came his way, may have caused Wilson to cool on his hunky movie star hopeful to focus on newer arrivals in his stable.

"I should have listened to him (Wilson). He knew what the fuck he was talking about! That was my big, dumb move that put me on the wrong course. He wanted me to be a movie star and I became a television actor. He knew what he was doing. He was a genius as an agent. If I had any brains, I would have listened to him. I wanted to work. But he wanted me to wait for 'that movie role'. He was right."

Regardless, there was no question that H.M. continued to get booked regularly on the small screen. The decade ended not only with nonstop work in 1959 single episodes of classics like *Peter Gunn, Maverick,* and the first season of *The Untouchables,* but also a second *Mike Hammer, Bat Masterson, M Squad* starring Lee Marvin, *Hudson's Bay* starring Barry Nelson, *Hawaiian Eye* starring Robert Conrad and Connie Stevens, and *Special Agent 7.*

H.M.'s career was doing so well that the entire family moved up into the Hollywood Hills to a 5-bedroom Spanish villa at 2562 Outpost Drive, valued in 2024 at over five million dollars.

There are a few key shows and roles in 1959 where H.M. shined, delivering on his Broadway-honed acting chops.

In March, H.M. starred in a memorable and moving episode of *One Step Beyond*, a supernaturally-themed half-hour anthology series on ABC that beat CBS's similar *The Twilight Zone* to the small screen by ten months. It even offered up host John Newland as the weekly "guide into the world of the unknown" who, like Rod Serling, would both introduce and close each episode with wise and piquant observations.

In "The Vision" (Season One, Episode 10), H.M. played one of three French soldiers during World War 1 who becomes mesmerized by a stationary, glowing light in the sky, so much so that the three soldiers all wordlessly drop their guns and walk off the battlefield. Court-martialed as deserters, the men (*Bonanza*'s Pernell Roberts among them) explain that they each truly believed they had left the battlefield for a place of peace (a family gathering, the deck of a ship, etc.) where, to quote H.M.'s Private Lacoste, holding a gun "felt obscene". Regardless, the three men are sentenced to be executed. Fortunately, without a moment to spare, word comes that enemy Russian soldiers have had the exact same experience. The execution is called off and John Newland informs us that this is "one version" of a true story where a genuine miracle took place and thousands of soldiers on both sides refused to kill.

As in *Playhouse 90*'s "Nightmare at Ground Zero", H.M.'s Private Lacoste is the one soldier of the trio with roguish charm, the only one with a sly smile and sense of humor, who desires only to get back home to his wine cellar.

Soon after, H.M. was back in the Wild West as the ruthless "comanchero" (or trader), Jonas Lester, in a Season One episode of the soon-to-be-hit series, *Rawhide*, which launched young Clint Eastwood to stardom. Recalled H.M.:

"I was the villain and it was Clint's episode that week. I captured him and beat the living hell out of him. At the end, they're firing at us, I run away, and he shoots me in the back. Forty years later, I worked with his daughter, Alison, in *The Philadelphia Story* on stage in Los Angeles."

As the episode's bad guy, soon to give Clint Eastwood a good beating for messing with his gal in *Rawhide*.

H.M. closed out the 1950's with his sixth and final episode of *Playhouse 90*, "Target for Three", the first episode of the much-lauded anthology show's fourth and final season. H.M. played Tomás, one of the three men indicated in the title, who are orchestrating the assassination of the ruthless dictator of a fictitious South American country. Ricardo Montalban, the leader, chooses George C. Scott, an unassuming but smart and cynical doctor, and H.M.'s Tomás, a smooth, playboy, restaurant musician with a paternity suit against him. Tomás is chosen because he's such a cad that no one would suspect him of being a part of a noble three-man assassination plot.

The episode is tautly written by David Davidson and impeccably orchestrated by director Robert Stephens, with maximum use of the soundstage to create interiors, exteriors, multilevel sets, moving jeeps, both day and night scenes, and even crowd scenes with gunfire, all broadcast live on October 1, 1959.

The three men are often positioned in uninterrupted three-shots, with intense dialogue flowing, and it is clear that H.M. is holding his own with these two charismatic heavyweights. Later, before his heroic self-sacrifice, he has a long scene with Scott in two-shot where H.M.'s Tomás nobly takes charge as Scott can only watch in admiration for the sort of selflessness Scott himself is likely incapable.

Screen grabs from one of H.M.'s very best roles and performances, as Tomás, the only one of the three would-be political assassins to make the ultimate sacrifice in *Playhouse 90's* "Target for Three". Pictured with Ricardo Montalban and George C. Scott.

This nuanced performance should have launched H.M. into the next tier. Unfortunately, it does not appear that H.M. was being well "protected" by his reps at this time. All publicity photos from the episode show only Montalban, Scott, and the female lead, Marisa Pavan, inaccurately inferring that they are the "Three" implied by the title. Adding insult to injury, H.M. did not receive mention in the series' coveted front marquee credit ("Tonight's episode stars…"), relegated instead to the tail credits.

Was Henry Wilson right when he suggested H.M. was cheapening his value by appearing in so many TV shows? "I made a lot of the wrong moves at that time. I just said yes. I wanted to work," said H.M. with obvious regret.

While "Target for Three" was not a wrong move in any sense of the term, one could argue that any acting credibility he achieved by appearing in it may have been undercut by simultaneously agreeing to appear in two episodes of the fairly silly *Men into Space* as Major Joe Hale. His second episode, "First Woman on the Moon", is a particular camp classic as Joe's wife, Renza (Nancy Gates) is brought on as one of the crew, a development with which Joe is uncomfortable. Unfortunately for the Women's Movement, Renza's duties are relegated to rocket housekeeping, cooking, and serving the men coffee.

Men Into Space also offered a rather bizarre footnote to

H.M.'s filmography, as H.M. explained: "Somewhere around 1969 or '70, I got a check in the mail for the first episode. I was truly confused, so I called someone at the Screen Actors Guild. It turns out they used a long clip of me from that show on a movie screen in the sleazy 42nd Street Theater where Bob Balaban fellates Jon Voight in *Midnight Cowboy*! There's my face, right between them, just before he goes down on Voight."

So as H.M. closed out the 1950's, he had not only appeared in a Tony Award winner for Best Play and an Emmy Award-winner for Best TV Production, but inadvertently found his way into the X-rated Academy Award winner for Best Picture of 1969!

And yet immortality was just around the corner…

Chapter Eight

THE TWILIGHT ZONE (1960)

Achieving immortality in a television classic.

"To me it was just another gig.
I had no idea it was going to be a marvelous show."

Just as H.M. ended the 1950's strong, he began the 1960's busier than ever. Among his many 1960 TV appearances were more episodes of *Gunsmoke*, *Bat Masterson*, and *M Squad* (playing different characters from those he had performed the previous season), plus a second episode of *One Step Beyond*, effectively starring as a low-class, charming murderer who stalks his prey in the park but is thwarted by the ghost of his intended victim's husband.

He also appeared in *77 Sunset Strip*, two episodes of Season Eight of *Death Valley Days*, *Hong Kong* starring Rod Taylor, which ran for one season, as well as *The Deputy*, a half-hour western series co-created by 38-year-old Norman Lear which was to be Henry Fonda's one and only foray into headlining a TV series.

On March 27, 1960, H.M. appeared in what would be his last live TV drama: an episode of *General Electric Theater* entitled "The Web of Guilt", hosted by Ronald Reagan, starring Arthur

Kennedy. After over a decade, the demanding real-time format had given way to successful, filmed three-camera sitcoms and one-hour TV dramas.

But on November 11, 1960, CBS broadcast a television episode in which H.M. had the lead, the role he is best remembered for: David Ellington, in the second season *The Twilight Zone* classic, "The Howling Man".

Ellington opens the episode as an older man, insisting that the story he is about to tell may sound impossible, but "You Must Believe!" We flashback 40 years to Ellington caught in a storm while on a post-World War 1 "walking tour" of Europe.

As host Rod Serling explains, from a script by Charles Beaumont, directed by Douglas Heyes, "The prostrate form of Mr. David Ellington, scholar, seeker of truth and, regrettably, finder of truth. A man who will shortly arise from his exhaustion to confront a problem that has tormented mankind since the beginning of time. A man who has knocked on a door seeking sanctuary and found instead, the outer edges of *The Twilight Zone*."

Hungry and exhausted, Ellington seeks refuge in a monastery run by "The Brotherhood of Truth" with the elder Brother Jerome (John Carradine) as their leader. Given his condition, Ellington is permitted to stay the night but is warned to pay no heed to the howling he may hear from behind a locked door. Brother

Jerome explains that it is the Devil himself they have captured and as long as he remains incarcerated, there will be no more war or cruelty upon the earth.

Unfortunately, this only intensifies Ellington's curiosity, who speaks to Jerome's captive (Robin Hughes) through the barred door. The captive explains the monks are mad and that he is merely a man whom they have decided is the Devil. Ellington is persuaded by their captive to open the door. The captive does indeed reveal himself to be The Devil, and escapes. When the episode returns to the present, we see that Ellington has been explaining all this to a new housekeeper, informing her (and us) that he has spent his life searching for the Devil and has finally re-captured him. In fact, he is in the very closet that they are both standing before. As Ellington leaves for evening plans, the curious housekeeper's hand moves closer and closer to the staff-shaped bolt that keeps the Howling Man at bay…

As Serling/Beaumont concludes, "Ancient folk saying: 'You can catch the Devil, but you can't hold him long.' Ask Brother Jerome. Ask David Ellington. They know, and they'll go on knowing to the end of their days and beyond — in *The Twilight Zone*."

Twenty years before the writing of this book, H.M. would recall the experience in great detail at the "Stars of the Twilight

Zone Convention" panel discussion,[3] held in August 2004 at the Beverly Garland Holiday Inn in Los Angeles, which I attended.

"*The Twilight Zone* is scheduled for five days — two days of rehearsing and three days of shooting. We had John Carradine in this cast, so the two days of rehearsal was a quick read-through of the script, and John Carradine, for the next two days, telling stories."

Recently, H.M. further elaborated, "Carradine told a story about an early screen test he was asked to do. He was told to emerge from behind a door and face the camera with a big smile, pause, and lick his lips repeatedly with great satisfaction before exiting frame. When Carradine was shown the finished screen test, after he exited frame, John Barrymore came out of the same door right after him and zipped up his fly. The whole screen test was a practical joke!"

Returning to the 2004 panel, H.M. explained how he came to be cast in it: "There was a kiddie park on Beverly Boulevard and La Cienega, with pony rides, and little dodge 'em cars, and a small little rollercoaster. My kids were on the rollercoaster and next to me was Doug Heyes, and we said hello to each other."

H.M. and Heyes had worked on many of the same shows

[3]Transcript courtesy of Andrew Ramage and The Twilight Zone Museum, as reprinted in The Twilight Zone Encyclopedia by Steven Jay Rubin, Chicago Review Press.

H.M. in *The Twilight Zone* where Brother Jerome (John Carradine) cautions him to never listen to the captured Devil's cries for release.

H.M. in old age makeup, insisting to his housekeeper, and the viewer: "You must believe!"

(*Cheyenne*, *M Squad*, *Maverick*, *Hawaiian Eye*), as actor and director, respectively, but never at the same time.

As H.M. continued in 2004, "The next day I get a call that I have this job. Obviously it was on his mind that he was doing this project, and he saw me and thought I would be good for this, and I got the part."

As the wanderer, David Ellington, who finds himself in a monastery where the monks just may have caught the Devil (Robin Hughes). *The Twilight Zone*: "The Howling Man".

Heyes utilized stylized visual techniques to convey Ellington's state of mind, as H.M. explained in 2004, "In order to show and accentuate the delirium of the man, Doug Heyes tilted the camera in the opposite direction of the way the man was always going, because he wanted to present the man as being delirious. It was a great gimmick, and rather new for the time."

H.M. went on to detail a critical creative tension on set between Heyes and writer, Charles Beaumont, who was thirty at the time, already a celebrated author of science fiction stories, and had penned some of the series' best episodes. He would die at age thirty-eight from an undiagnosed brain disease he ignored which has been theorized as early onset Alzheimer's coupled with Pick's Disease.

According to H.M., "When I allowed the devil to escape, this is where Heyes and Beaumont began their disagreement about the script and how it was done. Beaumont always wanted the devil to come out as the bedraggled man, and run and be chased by Ellington. And as he goes over the wall, he's supposed to reach up and grab his foot, which is a cloven hoof. And that indicates that he is the devil and you never see him. But Doug Heyes said that he promised the audience that he was going to show them the devil, therefore he's going to show them the Devil!"

"The Howling Man" consistently shows up in Top 25 lists

of the best *Twilight Zone* episodes, including the Top Ten on *Entertainment Weekly* and Number 1 on *Hypebeast*. The first season of Stephen King's 2018 supernatural Hulu series, *Castle Rock*, not only feels inspired by Beaumont's scenario, but a clip of H.M's episode appears on star, Sissy Spacek's TV screen in an early episode, removing any doubt as to King's influence.

As H.M. summed up, "These are two rather talented men — Doug Heyes, the brilliant director who sees everything in images, like a painter, and Charles Beaumont, the writer, a brilliant writer. They argued about everything, and they gave into each other. And they turned out a marvelous piece of work."

Chapter Nine

THE SERIOUS SIXTIES (1960-1962)

Perry Mason, Wagon Train, and Route 66

"I made very little judgement. I just did the work."

H.M. has joked that the only hallmark of 1960's television in which he inexplicably did not appear was *Bonanza*. A close examination of his filmography would concur.

By 1960, *Perry Mason* was in its fourth season and still a major hit. Known for Raymond Burr playing Erle Stanley Gardner's fictitious defense attorney, part of the fun each week was seeing Mason pitted against fine actor, William Talman, as Mason's key rival in the courtroom: District Attorney Hamilton Burger. But on March 12, 1960, police raided 1156 N. Curson Avenue in Hollywood and arrested eight people on "morals charges", purportedly engaged in a "nude marijuana party," according to the Los Angeles Mirror-News (March 14, 1960) where officers found "dirty movies, spicy books, and lewd photos."

CBS fired the popular Talman based on the arrest alone and brought in a few different actors to play the D.A., one of whom was H.M. playing Deputy D.A. Sampson in three episodes. H.M. had already appeared in two episodes as different characters and recalled of Talman, "Bill would sit at his prosecutor's table, smoking during breaks in the shooting, then put the cigarette in an ashtray hidden in his desk. After they'd cut, he'd take out the cigarette. He died of lung cancer. But he was a wonderful guy and actor. Unbelievably good in *The Hitch Hiker*."

Talman and the others were eventually cleared of all charges resulting in Talman being brought back to the show as D.A. Burger, much to Burr and the producers' delight, who had stood by him. As for H.M., he would appear in five more episodes (ten total in all but one of the show's nine seasons), in five different roles, making him the only actor to appear on *Perry Mason* as a prosecutor, defendant, murder victim, witness, and murderer!

"Raymond Burr was a friend of the family. He and Ethel went to acting school together at the Pasadena Playhouse before she moved to New York to work in the theater," recalled H.M.

By this point, Ethel's behind-the-scenes Television career was also on the rise. An unapologetic workaholic, she settled at CBS where she steadily moved through the executive ranks based on her uncanny ability to spot talent and work effectively with major directors. It was not, however, as it is today, where network television has many female executives, Vice Presidents, and Heads of Programing. Back then, Ethel Winant (she and their children maintained the original spelling) was one of the only female executives at the three big networks, having to cater to, and answer to, the men. At the height of her powers, in the 1970's, she would be responsible for selecting the casts of such iconic shows as *All in the Family* and *The Mary Tyler Moore Show*, becoming the very first female Vice President at any major network.

But despite Ethel's success, she had very little to do with H.M.'s hiring for shows at CBS. According to H.M., "Ethel was firmly against nepotism. She was so anti-nepotism that sometimes she actually stood in the way of family and friends getting jobs!" Later, she would admit to family members that it was from a fear that she would not be taken seriously at CBS if she tried to get work for family members or close friends.

H.M., Ethel, and the three boys at Knott's Berry Farm, circa 1960.

With both parents working all day, and with Ethel never getting a driver's license, H.M. and Ethel hired Fred Gonzalez, a live-in driver/nanny/chef on Monday through Friday, to drive Ethel to and from work, take care of the house, and cook for the boys, including dinner which they would eat long before their parents got home at 7pm. But whereas H.M. could leave his work behind when he walked through the door, Ethel planted herself attentively in front of the TV in the master bedroom to watch her own network and keep tabs on the competition. Ultimately, H.M. was the warmer and more approachable of the two parents.

"He was a great dad," recalled youngest son, Bruce, "taking us to playgrounds and parks." Saturday night was the one night the family would have dinner together, with Ethel cooking her one meal of the week: leg of lamb. Despite H.M.'s love of the creative arts — acting, dance, singing, and later, sculpting — he freely admitted he never gravitated towards cooking. On Sundays, H.M. insisted he drive the family to the beach, to which Ethel agreed, while toting an armful of scripts.

"At the beach, Dad would play with us, but Mom read scripts," remembered Bruce.

As 1960 drew to a close, H.M. appeared on a New Year's Eve episode of *Shotgun Slade* ("Ring of Death") playing a particularly nasty lead villain with one especially powerhouse dramatic scene opposite stage actress Bethel Leslie.

"I've played a lot of evil people," H.M. recalled on *A Word on Westerns* in a 2018 interview with Rob Word, "and that was probably the most evil person I ever played. Bethel Leslie, a wonderful actress, is wearing a ring that will incriminate me in the murder of her fiancé. I meet with her privately, see she's wearing the ring, I get so angry that I strangle her to death. And then I threw her over the cliff!"

H.M. ushered in 1961 with the last of his three D.A. Sampson turns in *Perry Mason* as well as a pair of solid *Wagon Train* episodes in two different roles. In "The Nellie Jefferson Story," H.M. played a henpecked manager of the strong-willed titular

As D.A. Sampson for three episodes of *Perry Mason* after series regular, William Talman, was temporarily suspended on a morals charge. Raymond Burr seated in background. H.M. would ultimately appear in a total of ten episodes; the only actor on the show to ever play a prosecutor, defendant, murder victim, witness, and murderer!

stage actress (Janis Paige) who's got a dark past she's hiding. His larger role was as Jason Powers in that same year's "The Selena Hartwell Story". In it, Jason and the vengeful Selena (Jan Sterling) are a pair of incognito bounty hunters looking to bring accused killer, Will Cotrell (Claude Akins), to justice. Jason has long been pining for Selena, who only has room in her heart for hate and revenge, because Will killed a man she loved in self-defense. In the climax, Selena and Jason are accompanying the bound Will to justice but are ambushed by a trio of bandits. Jason is shot trying to defend Selena, but Will is freed by the badmen who insist Will kill his female captor. Will chooses to take on the trio instead, nearly losing his life before help arrives. Selena tearfully sees Jason die in her arms, after which she decides to move on from vengeance, giving Will a second chance at life with his ten-year-old son.

But it was in the most unlikeliest of places that H.M. had one of his very best TV roles: *The Loretta Young Show*. "Unlikely" because the anthology show, already in its eighth season, was well-known as a showcase for its movie star hostess, who nearly always played the central role.

"My first episode for the show was called 'Quiet Desperation' and it's one of the very few episodes of *The Loretta Young Show* where she didn't have the lead. I did."

The title was derived from the Thoreau quote: "The mass of

men lead lives of quiet desperation."

Airing three months after H.M.'s *Twilight Zone* episode, it was a very early directing effort by Richard Donner, who would go on to helm *The Omen, Superman,* and *Lethal Weapon.* H.M. played Victor Perkins, a businessman and father whose boss wants to transfer him (and therefore his family) to Japan. Victor is in a rut and feels the move will reinvigorate his feelings about himself and about life. His wife, Linda (Young), panics, refusing to go, for no other reason than she is resistant to change. With the couple on the verge of a breakup, Victor acquiesces, but it is clear his spirit has been killed. Once Linda realizes this, and faces her own fears, she supports Victor and they do, in fact, make the big move.

H.M.'s Victor is one of his most anguished, yet understated performances. Although only 33 at the time, with grey added to his temples, H.M. convinces the viewer that he is middle-aged and much more world-weary. We believe that this scary move is his last chance at an exciting career. Loretta Young was 14 years older than H.M., yet they make an evenly matched married couple, both here and in their subsequent pairing in the episode "Not in Their Stars", which aired four months later. In that episode, Young played a wife ruled by her obsession with horoscopes and fortune-tellers. Her husband (H.M.) at first tries to placate her, but when her "addiction" gets destructive, he tries to get her to see her folly.

Fortunately, fate lends a hand and all ends happily.

Of Loretta Young, H.M. recalled, "She's the first one who dragged me to the dailies. Insisted! 'You've got to go to the dailies because that's where you really *learn*,' she said."

Although it is unclear who was representing H.M. at the time, they should have continued to only book H.M. in roles that showcased him as a lead or major support, as was the case with many of his peers. Unfortunately, only two weeks after his lead on *The Loretta Young Show*, H.M. appeared in a minor supporting role that was beneath him, as a goofball short order cook in an episode of the Boris Karloff-hosted *Thriller*, entitled "The Fingers of Death".

The following year, 1962, was filled with work in shows largely forgotten today — *Cain's Hundred*, *Outlaws*, *Target: The Corruptors!*, *The Eleventh Hour* — as well as two more episodes of *Hawaiian Eye*, and the first of two episodes of *Cheyenne*, starring Clint Walker.

He played an amputee Korean War veteran in the first season of the successful E.G. Marshall / Robert Reed legal drama, *The Defenders* (working again for director Franklin Schaffner). The episode is also distinguished by marking the on-screen debut of Gene Wilder, playing a waiter who serves H.M. and his fellow war veterans who have gathered, ostensibly, for a reunion but, in truth, to try one of the six (Lee Philips) for an act of treason.

Other notables did creep up in '62, like a decent role in his third *Gunsmoke* episode, Season Seven's "The Do-Badder", which aired on January 6th. But it was in March of that year where H.M. had one of his most unique roles, and the first time he would play into his Judaism, in an episode of *Route 66* entitled, "Shoulder the Sky, My Lad".

"Ed Asner is killed and I played his rabbi who had to console his son and convince him to go on with his bar mitzvah," remembered H.M. "I had to do the kaddish over his grave. Ed taught me the kaddish phonetically the day before."

With E.G. Marshall as an amputee Korean War veteran in *The Defenders*.

Despite the religious home in which Haim was raised, as an adult he did not gravitate towards orthodoxy in his Jewish faith. He did, however, enjoy and take part in the culture of Judaism.

"My parents were religious but never forced it on any of us. I got bar mitzvah'd at age 50 in Israel in 1977. I was at a basketball game and there was a rabbi sitting next to me. He talked me into it! Shirley Jones threw me a bar mitzvah party when I got home."

But more on H.M. and his special friendship with Shirley Jones later…

As 1962 drew to a close, after appearances on *Dr. Kildare* and another good heavy role in *The Untouchables*, H.M. found himself on a movie set for the first time in five years… opposite the biggest rock and roll star of all time.

Chapter Ten

The Cinematic Sixties (1962-1965)

Back on the big screen with Elvis Presley, Ann Bancroft, and James Garner

I wanted to keep working because eventually,
every day you wait becomes a week, every week a month.
You destroy yourself."

In 1962, Elvis Presley had a Number 1 hit song with "Good Luck Charm" and a Number 2 hit song with "Return to Sender". His biggest movie hit to that point was 1961's *Blue Hawaii*, but grosses fell off for his next two films.

In the Fall of 1962, it was decided that maybe it was time to show the warm and fuzzy side of The King of Rock and Roll by putting him in a movie that allowed him to interact with a cute kid. And so *It Happened at the World's Fair* went into production in Seattle on September 5th in order to shoot some key scenes at the actual World's Fair, which took place there from April 21 to October 21. The rest was shot at MGM and the film was released the following year on April 3, 1963.

"Elvis was a consummate actor," H.M. recalled. "I remember that the director (Oscar-winner, Norman Taurog, helming his fourth Elvis movie) said, 'The leading men are all shits. It's the character actors who are really nice.' But Elvis wasn't a shit. He was wonderful."

Elvis plays Mike Edwards, who flies a crop duster with his buddy, Danny (*2001*'s Gary Lockwood). Unfortunately, Danny has a gambling problem, and his debts have caused the sheriff to seize their plane. The two buddies hitchhike to the World's Fair in Seattle to make some money. While Danny swears he won't gamble any more, Mike stumbles into having to take care of a young girl, Sue-Lin (Vicky Tiu), whose Uncle Walter (Kam Tong) has disappeared. Along the way (and this being an Elvis movie), Elvis

As slick hood, Vince Bradley, holding a gun on the principal cast of *It Happened at the World's Fair* (1962). From left: H.M., Gary Lockwood, Joan O'Brien, Elvis Presley. Vicky Tiu in foreground.

finds himself smitten by Diane, a young nurse who is working at the fair's first aid office (Joan O'Brien, fresh from starring opposite Jerry Lewis in Frank Tashlin's *It's Only Money*). The more resistant Diane is to Elvis's charms, the more he is determined to woo her, often via song.

While the movie shows us "Singing Elvis" (ten songs as Elvis wanders the fair, strumming his guitar), "Romantic Elvis", and "Daddy Elvis" as reluctant but charming protector to adorable Sue-Lin, the movie also makes time for "Rough and Tumble Elvis", made possible by Danny's gambling problem. Danny has not only found himself a poker game in Seattle (breaking his vow to not gamble), but he's also considering taking a fast money gig from a slick, local hood, Vince Bradley (H.M.), to get their plane out of hock, which Elvis cautions against.

In the climax, the two pals realize that Vince has secretly stashed stolen furs inside their plane so that they can unwittingly smuggle them out of the country for him. When they refuse, Vince pulls a gun, which cues Sue-Lin to bite H.M.'s hand, causing him to drop the pistol. With no gun, and Danny knocked out, Elvis and H.M. engage in one of Elvis's best on-screen fist fights.

"It took eight or nine hours to shoot the one-minute fight scene," detailed H.M. "It was beautifully choreographed. All the hits were perfect. You never saw air between the hit and the hand.

When you're working with Elvis, you better be on your guard because he's really swinging! The stunt men set it up but it's mostly Elvis and me. This was the case in most of my fight scenes. I was a dancer, so I could follow the precise fight choreography. That said, the next morning I woke up completely sore everywhere!"

The climactic fistfight in *It Happened at the World's Fair*. H.M. fought dirty, but The King still ruled.

Tales have been told of Elvis's impulsive generosity, and H.M. found himself on the receiving end. "I admired his Rolex so he took it off and handed it to me. Can you believe that? And like an idiot, I lost it! I was doing something at my car and took it off to protect it. I think I put it on the hood. Then I drove off and realized I had left it on the car! It was gone! The Rolex Elvis gave me!"

Two months before the film's release, H.M. worked again at MGM, now for director Arthur Hiller, who had directed him eight years earlier in his first *Playhouse 90*. It was a big, glossy, romantic comedy called *The Wheeler Dealers*, akin to the popular Rock Hudson / Doris Day films, this time with James Garner and Lee Remick. It had a wonderful supporting cast (Jim Backus, Louis Nye, Phil Harris, Chill Wills, and John Astin), but it is a rugged H.M. in a sleeveless shirt, rolling a cigarette, that is the very first, pre-credit, widescreen, Cinemascope shot after the MGM logo as Bo Bluedog, oil contractor, whose operation falls prey to conman James Garner's deliberately bungled oil well speculation. But, unfortunately, H.M. is not in the film beyond this scene. In the end, it was the sort of role the insatiably work-hungry H.M. was prone to accept but, in terms of "bigger picture" career management, should not have taken as it likely lessened his value.

After *World's Fair* opened in April of '63, it did not instantly roll H.M. back into a feature career after his TV-fueled five-year hiatus. Ultimately, H.M. was back on small screens in 1963 in the one and only season of *Temple Houston*, starring Jeffrey Hunter (later to star as the pre-Shatner Captain in the pilot for *Star Trek*). 1963's episode of *Arrest and Trial* ("Inquest into a Bleeding Heart") would also be the first time he appeared onscreen with actor and later, best friend, Richard Basehart, whom H.M. would build a live theater for in the 1980's in the San Fernando Valley and name in his honor, but more on that to come. His eighth episode of *Perry Mason* was broadcast in '63, this time featuring H.M. as a corrupt Assistant College Dean who becomes the episode's murder victim.

In 1964, H.M. had a seven-episode run on the ABC daytime soap opera, *The Young Marrieds*, but as it was opposite CBS's hit, *Edge of Night*, the series lasted less than two years. However, other than an episode of *Combat!* starring Vic Morrow, and a fifth episode of *Gunsmoke* (and a sixth shortly after) it was an atypically quiet year.

In the summer of 1965, H.M. found himself on the Paramount lot with front credit billing in the cast of one of the highest pedigreed films of his career: *The Slender Thread*. It starred Sidney Poitier and Anne Bancroft, both recent Best Actor/Actress Oscar winners, under the direction of 31-year-old Sydney Pollack making his feature film directing debut after helming multiple episodes of many of the hit TV shows of the early 1960's.

If one were to look at The Internet Movie Database's listing for *The Slender Thread*, it appears that H.M.'s role as Doctor Morris is significant. His image is the key photo for the listing and he also appears in the trailer. Unfortunately, his association with the movie proved such a disappointment that he has no memory of making it nor of his intense scene opposite Bancroft, hot off her Best Actress win for *The Miracle Worker*.

Taking place in real time, the movie is centered on Poitier as a suicide hotline operator who has the recently overdosed Bancroft on the other end of the line. With the clock ticking for her lethal drug intake to claim her life, Poitier plays an intense game of phone detective, which includes flashbacks to Bancroft's emotionally trying last few days. Among those flashbacks is Bancroft unsuccessfully seeking psychological counseling at the hospital where H.M. appears as a suited, late-night intern on his dinner break who meets with Bancroft in the waiting area, ultimately unable to help her. The camera remains on Bancroft's face for nearly the entire anguished scene and, frankly, why shouldn't it? Hers is the intense lead role while Dr. Morris is there to listen patiently and try to calm her.

Nevertheless, going to see the movie when it premiered was still exciting for H.M.… until he watched the front credits and saw he was mistakenly billed as "H.N. Wynant", which studios are not obligated to correct. As H.M. recalled, "That's the one thing I can remember about that picture: sitting in a theater with family and friends and being totally embarrassed when my name appeared on screen misspelled. It had never happened before and there was nothing I could do about it."

Ultimately, the film was nominated for two Oscars (Costumes and Art Direction) and received a Golden Globe nomination for its taut screenplay.

Around this time, H.M. and Ethel's three boys were 8, 11, and 12, and loved to play outside, especially riding their bikes. The

Portrait, circa 1962, with his three sons: oldest William, youngest Bruce, and middle son Scott.

increasingly busy canyon road of Outpost Drive in the Hollywood Hills made bike-riding virtually impossible. So, the family packed up and decided to move to a more kid-friendly neighborhood in the flat, less trafficked streets of L.A.'s Westwood neighborhood, walking distance from trendy Westwood Village and UCLA.

1965 also brought two more *Perry Mason* episodes (again playing new characters each time), bringing his final episode tally to ten. In Season Two of *The Fugitive*, H.M. was a scar-faced assassin named Pinto. His climactic fist fight with star David Janssen is shot mostly in long shot with stunt men, but for the close shots of the two actors, one of Janssen's punches accidentally connected.

"He caught me right on the nose and felt horrible about it,"

With Ross Martin in *The Wild, Wild West.*

recalled H.M. "I kept telling him it was all right, but he was an emotional wreck for the rest of the day."

The busy year continued with his sixth appearance on *Gunsmoke*, a three-part episode of *Branded* with Chuck Connors (which was later edited into a single movie entitled *Broken Sabre* and released internationally), his first of four episodes of *The Wild, Wild West* (always in a different role), and NBC's Peabody Award winning, historical, scripted anthology series, *Profiles in Courage*. There could be no question that H.M. was living the life he had sought: that of a working character actor, living one gig to the next, with little design or discretion other than consistent employment.

Chapter Eleven

THE PSYCHEDELIC SIXTIES (1966-1969)

Batman, I Spy, The Wild Wild West, The Man from U.N.C.L.E., Mission: Impossible, and Get Smart!

I kept working and working. There were other very talented actors out here from New York, many of them were my friends from the theater, but they weren't working. I felt guilty as shit. You have no idea!"

1966 brought two more episodes of *The Wild, Wild West*, the second of which, "Night of the Sudden Plague", provided H.M. a good lead villain as Coley Rodman, leader of bank robbers who are partnered with a mad scientist in a genre mashup that was the series' frequent signature. H.M. had another solid role in a three-

As Frosty, the Number 1 henchman to Eli Wallach's Mister Freeze in a *Batman* two-parter.

part episode of *Branded* entitled "Call to Glory", which was later re-edited into a theatrical feature retitled *Blade Rider - Revenge of the Indian Nations* for international release.

1967 proved to be one of H.M.'s most iconic years, appearing in four of the most important American TV shows in terms of influence on the pop culture of the 1960's and beyond: *Batman, I Spy, The Man from U.N.C.L.E.*, and *Get Smart*.

For *Batman*, H.M. appeared in two consecutive episodes — "Ice Spy" and "The Duo Defy" — as gleefully villainous chief henchman, Frosty, to Eli Wallach's Mr. Freeze. Wallach was the third star to essay the icy iconic "guest villain" in the successful ABC series, following George Sanders and Otto Preminger. "We had a very well-trained seal on that set. We all treated it like a puppy dog," remembered H.M. "It was fun to work with Eli again, who I knew from New York. He had taken over for the role of Sakini in *Teahouse* on Broadway. On the set,

Mr. Feeze and Frosty giving Elisha Cook, Jr. (seated) a hard time.

I remember he'd scream 'Ice Men! To the Attack!' and then the stunt men would step in and do all the fighting!"

H.M.'s *The Man from U.N.C.L.E.* was also a two-parter in which he played not one but four roles! "The Prince of Darkness Affair," featured a mustachioed H.M. as all four Aksoy Brothers (Hasan, Omar, Karim, and Ali), who appear one at a time. The gag — and it's a good one — is that as each Aksoy brother is killed, the next mustachioed revenge-seeking sibling appears to take his place. The first is a gruff, no nonsense, mute knife-thrower, but in the last scene, the final Aksoy (Ali) is well-spoken and charming,

Having a tour de force in a two-parter of *The Man from U.N.C.L.E.*, playing all four Aksoy Brothers. Here, in the finale, he may just get the girl (Carol Lynley) while star Robert Vaughn looks on.

walking off with guest star Carol Lynley as her potential, happily-ever-after love interest. It not only offered H.M. a little tour de force within the two episodes, but three death scenes! The two one-hour episodes were edited together and released as a single movie the next year through MGM, incongruently retitled, *The Helicopter Spies*.

The *I Spy* episode, "Apollo", featured a bespectacled H.M. as tech-savvy saboteur, Manfred, who together with fellow enemy agent, Bobbie (*Auntie Mame's* Pippa Scott), plan to blowup a NASA test site. It was a strong, fast-paced episode that earned its journeyman series director, Earl Bellamy, a Directors Guild of America Award nomination, and was lent a particular authenticity by being shot on location in Lost Hills, California, at the Santa Susanna Labs amidst real NASA equipment. Forty years later, H.M. and Pippa Scott would be reunited with major roles in the independently produced feature film, *Footprints* (shot in 2007, released in 2011), though not on screen at the same time. For more on that title, see Chapter 18.

In one of H.M.'s few forays into series comedy, he was the main villain in the "Pussycats Galore" episode of *Get Smart* as Frank Valentine, clearly inspired by Hugh Hefner, the owner of a night club whose waitresses all dress as "pussycats". Valentine secretly uses the club as a venue for smuggling and kidnapping.

As the bad-guy owner of the Pussycat Club in *Get Smart*, a rare foray into series comedy. From left: Don Adams, Ted Knight (as H.M.'s henchman), and Barbara Feldon.

Smart (Don Adams) and Agent 99 (Barbara Feldon) go undercover as sought-after German scientists. Valentine and Ted Knight, playing Valentine's Number One flunky, are not only outsmarted by Smart, but by CONTROL Agent Watkins in a daring bit of casting. Watkins, male, is introduced as a female impersonator and is played by the female and voluptuous Angelique Pettyjohn. The episode gets a lot of subversive mileage from Watkins flirting with Agent 99 (who seems alternately put-off and turned-on) and Smart, who makes no bones about his attraction to Watkins.

That same busy year, after completing an episode of *The Virginian* with Leslie Nielsen, H.M. went on location to Nashville where casting director and soon-to-be good friend, Marvin Paige (who had worked with H.M. on *Branded*, *Combat!*, and *The Young Marrieds*), was putting together back-to-back features to be shot consecutively for Tennessee-based Baptist pastor and fledgling movie producer, E. Stanley Williamson, for his Ambassador Films shingle. Williamson helped legitimize his Nashville operation by bringing in veteran director, Joseph Kane (age 73 at the time) for a three-picture deal. Kane had directed his first feature 32 years earlier — *Tumbling Tumbleweeds* with Gene Autry. He continued on at Republic Pictures for many years, including over twenty Roy Rogers films and five starring John Wayne. Paige and Kane wanted H.M. for roles in the second and third film on the Ambassador slate.

First up for H.M. was *Track of Thunder*, released by United Artists. Shot in Cinemascope in and around Fairground

With Leslie Nielsen on a 1967 episode of *The Virginian*.

Speedways, the film centered on a long-established but financially ailing "mom 'n' pop" box-car raceway that was now taken over for the syndicate by big city gangster, Maxwell Carstairs, played by H.M. sporting a sharply groomed villain mustache. With raceway attendance low, Carstairs decides to drum up crowds by creating a rivalry between his two star drivers, played by Tommy Kirk (who later admitted in an interview, "I was fooling around with drugs at the time so I was about half awake in that film. I just sort of walked through it and took the money."[4]) and Ray Strickland, for the heart of Shelley (Brenda Benet, another actor Paige brought over from ABC's *The Young Marrieds*). Also legitimizing the regional film was Howard Hughes discovery and 1950's "scream queen", Faith Domergue, as Kirk's mother.

Carstairs is aided in his PR efforts by a local columnist, Georgia (Majel Barrett, wife of Gene Roddenbery), who is falling for Carstairs' insincere romantic charms. Carstairs also blackmails Kirk's mechanic Bowser (James Dobson) to aid him. When Carstairs orchestrates the explosion of Tommy's unmanned car and insinuates Ray's jealous complicity, Ray quits. Bowser fills in, driving against Tommy, and dying in a fiery crash. The two friends reconcile, with Tommy marrying Shelley with Ray's blessing, but not before jilted Georgia turns over evidence to the police, who

---

[4]Minton, Kevin, "Sex, Lies, and Disney Tape: Walt's Fallen Star", Filmfax Issue 38, April 1993 p 71.

arrest Carstairs at the speedway for embezzlement.

Shot quickly with undistinguished direction and cinematography, the editor was then unknown, future Oscar-winner, Verna Fields. Two years after she had cut the three films for Ambassador, she would begin editing a string of classics, including *Medium Cool*, *What's Up Doc?*, *Paper Moon*, *American Graffiti*, and *Jaws*, for which she won her Oscar. But even Fields had a difficult time constructing anything exciting from the limited shots provided to her for the racing sequences.

H.M.'s second movie for Ambassador, with most of the same team behind the camera, was in an entirely different arena. *The Search for the Evil One* is the only produced feature screenplay by Don Fearheighly and introduced fourth-billed H.M. as an unnamed Director of the OAS, based in Tel Aviv, who drafts US Agent Becker (an insistently stiff Lee Patterson, on his way to eleven years on soap opera, *One Life to Live*) to South America where Hitler (Pitt Herbert) is reported to be living in hiding and plotting the rise of the Fourth Reich. Becker is a Jew, whose real family name is Levy. Back in World War II, Becker's father was forced into aiding the Nazis in order to protect his family. He was betrayed and his family executed by real-life Nazi official, Martin Bormann (an effective Henry Brandon, who had played the villainous Barnaby in *March of the Wooden Soldiers* over 30 years earlier). As a boy, Becker managed to escape. After his father dies, Becker decides to accept the South American assignment to avenge his family. The good news is, the quite-mad Hitler is ultimately blown to bits just moments after Bormann meets the same fate.

Although H.M.'s charismatic, authoritative performance is confined to the film's first half-hour, this is nevertheless the more interesting, slightly better-made film of the two, which in no way is meant to imply it is a good film, only superior to *Track of Thunder*. However, of the two films, *The Search for the Evil One* is the far more elusive film to locate in its entirety. Unlike *Track of Thunder* (which, as of this writing, can be streamed on Amazon Prime Video, although not in the Cinemascope aspect ratio), it had a more splotchy theatrical release before vanishing into obscurity with only a 1988 VHS release, in terms of Home Entertainment.

Upon returning to Los Angeles, H.M. was back at work on his fourth and final episode of *The Wild, Wild West*: "Night of the Simian Terror", which aired in February 1968. Clearly inspired by Arthur Conan Doyle's *The Hound of the Baskervilles*, it provided H.M. with his last and juiciest role on the series as Aaron Buckley, the mysterious and wealthy member of the plagued Buckley family.

1968 was also notable for H.M.'s appearance on *The Vir-*

ginian as Sturdevant, a shady, big city businessman sent by a consortium of wealthy fur traders to offer guest star Ricardo Montalban $10,000 towards his planned revolution. This presents a moral dilemma for the righteous Montalban, resulting in some lengthy, powerful scenes between H.M. and his old friend, Montalban.

Two years after his tenth and final *Perry Mason*, H.M. was back on set with Ethel's old Pasadena Playhouse theater student friend, Raymond Burr, on the second season of Burr's new hit show, *Ironside*. The episode was "Side Pocket", with H.M. playing the ice-cold Phil Vance, who manipulates a young pool hustler in a match against an old pro (Jack Albertson). Vance is the sort of slick, self-assured, attractive gangster role, complete with a "cheap blonde on his arm" (here, Corinne Cole) that Richard Conte typified on the big screen in the 1955 film noir classic, *The Big Combo*. Here, H.M. delivers it with equal aplomb on the small screen, and in color no less.

"Jack Albertson was an excellent pool player. He did a lot of his own difficult shots," H.M. recalled with admiration. "I remember watching the actors and their stand-ins playing pool and thinking I used to beat every adult in the hall when I was a teenager back in Detroit."

The last notable role of 1968 was on the unfairly forgotten ABC one-hour World War II espionage series, *Garrison's Gorillas*, a fusion of *The Dirty Dozen* and *Hogan's Heroes* which also owed quite a bit to *Mission: Impossible* in its assignment-of-the-week structure and use of disguises and phony identities. H.M. had one of his most urbane and "cool" guest roles, as Duclos, the elegant owner of a French Casino, sharing a lot of screen time with Gena Rowlands who played a conwoman drafted into aiding Garrison (Ron Harper) and his team. In the end, trying to play both sides — Nazis and Garrison's Gorillas — Duclos' efforts to outsmart the Gorillas lands him on the wrong side of both the Nazis and a gun barrel. It was a well-produced show with lively chemistry amongst its ensemble cast, but unfortunately, it didn't have a breakout star in the mix to garner high enough ratings to keep the expensive period adventure show on the air beyond one season. It is interesting to note that when one compares H.M.'s sophisticated, charismatic Duclos with his enthusiastic, gleeful thug Frosty on *Batman*, his character actor range was never more apparent.

As 1969 began, H.M. revisited his Hollywood roots in the Western arena. First was an episode of *The Big Valley* as the smooth "Federale", Captain Chavez, who is determined to catch fellow guest star, Gerald Mohr as Dr. Mendez, a would-be revolutionary and current husband of the ex-girlfriend of series star, Lee Majors. In this episode's reimagining of *Casablanca* tropes, Mendez is Paul Henreid to Majors' Bogart. However, here the finale has H.M.'s Chavez (in the Claude Rains role) forced to justifiably shoot and kill Mendez in order to save Majors and then fabricate a false narrative that spares Mendez's reputation. It was a nice and complex little role, allowing H.M. a nuanced performance.

The second Western episode of the year gave H.M. his final onscreen appearance as a Native American, the Navajo, "Bear Hunter", in the last episode of the first and only season of ABC's *The Outcasts*. The show's progressive premise teamed a former Confederate soldier (Don Murray) with a former Union soldier who was also an ex-slave (Otis Young), as a pair of bounty hunters. H.M. had not donned a stock, black "Indian wig" in years and while his role is large and his performance strong, he is flanked throughout by actual Native American actors and extras, making it clear that this would be the last time H.M. essayed such a role. Playing a bare-chested "Indian" was what first brought Haim Winant from Broadway to Hollywood, and now - twelve years later - it was fitting that H.M. Wynant's final Native American role would have an on-screen death-by-stabbing at the hands of Otis Young, the second Black actor to have a series lead on a Western TV series.

In looking back on H.M.'s Native American roles throughout his career on both the big and small screen, one thing resonates without fault each time: he was hired to act a role, took it seriously, and portrayed the Native American character — whether hero or villain — with respect and dignity. There is no trace of caricature or condescension in H.M.'s interpretation, from *Run of the Arrow*'s Crazy Wolf through *The Outcasts*' Bear Hunter. So, while it is no longer accepted in the entertainment industry for non-Native Americans to don "red face", H.M. can look back proudly at the sensitive work he did in bringing the many varied and important stories of Native Americans to audiences worldwide.

His last significant TV role of the 1960's was in one of the decade's most beloved shows: *Mission: Impossible*. In the two-parter, "The Controllers", H.M. played Lorkner, part of a team of scientists for the baddies, but more lecherous than the others, with a hint of sadism injected into his role. His treatment of Brooke Bundy's captive patient, Katherine (Bundy was 25 at the time but made to appear much younger) is particularly unsettling, with both actors bringing a little unspoken mini-story to the proceedings with their glances, pauses, and reactions, beyond anything actually written in the script. H.M. also had the distinction of playing the character in the episode whose face is replicated as a flawless mask — a series hallmark — this time worn and removed with a flourish by Leonard Nimoy.

H.M. closed out the decade with his first major big screen role since trading punches with Elvis seven years earlier.

"I was at the airport picking up Ethel. Paul Bogart (a veteran TV director) was at the urinal next to me. We hadn't worked together but had crossed paths a number of times and worked on a lot of the same shows. 'Hi, H. How are you?' 'Fine, Paul. How are you?' Then we went our separate ways. The next day I got six weeks at MGM on *Marlowe* playing the heavy."

Bogart directed this first (and so far, only) contemporary film adaptation of Raymond Chandler's 1949 novel, *The Little Sister*, which was the movie's working title, including up through some early press materials. Adapted for the screen by Stirling Silliphant, who had just won the Oscar for his screenplay to *In the Heat of the Night*, it follows a traditional Raymond Chandler /

Making it clear to star, James Garner, that he should seriously reconsider his investigation in *Marlowe*.

Dashiell Hammett detective construct of what appear to be seemingly unrelated cases and clients that all ultimately converge as one twisted web of lies and manipulations, with private detective Philip Marlowe (James Garner) chief among the characters being deceived.

As with Garner's earlier MGM film, *The Wheeler Dealers*, H.M. once again is the first character we see, this time as part of a stylishly designed title credit sequence showing him making love poolside to the beautiful actress, Gayle Hunnicutt. We are seeing the images through the lens of an unseen photographer hiding in the bushes. It is that photographer (Jackie Coogan) who calls Marlowe to meet him but when the private eye arrives, he finds

In the opening credits, as mobster Sonny Steelgrave, seducing Gayle Hunnicutt, resulting in incriminating photos that are the McGuffin for *Marlowe* (1969).

the photographer has been murdered. As it turns out, Hunnicutt's character is a major TV star named Mavis Wald, who is having a clandestine affair with Sonny Steelgrave (H.M.), a notorious mobster. Those photos could ruin her career if the press ever got ahold of them.

An ensemble of colorful and shady characters come and go, including Mavis' exotic dancer friend Dolores (Rita Moreno), her high-strung little sister (Sharon Farrell), her shrink (Paul Stephens), and Carroll O'Connor playing bad cop to Kenneth Tobey's good cop. Marlowe describes H.M.'s Sonny Steelgrave as "dark, late thirties, slick, something for the ladies," and H.M. does not disappoint. He is a cool man of few words, who lets the fists and feet of his chief henchman, Winslow Wong (Bruce Lee), do the talking. Twenty-eight-year-old Lee is charming and funny, even when he decimates Marlowe's office while the detective remains seated

Studio portrait used for *Marlowe* press kit.

throughout. Lee was already a known TV figure from playing Kato in *The Green Hornet*, but he would ultimately make his mark as a leading man by walking away from Hollywood and its limitations for Asian actors and returning to Hong Kong to captain the feature film career that would lead him to screen legend status.

"He destroyed that office in one take! We were all in awe," H.M. remembered. As for Garner, with whom H.M. had worked on *Maverick* as well as *The Wheeler Dealers*, "James Garner was one of the guys. He was fun. He was a cool man. I knew him very well in New York. Even when he was an extra on Broadway — on stage as a juror, I believe — everybody knew he was going to be a huge star."

The movie seems to be building to a big showdown between Marlowe and Steelgrave but it is ultimately diverted. More's the pity because the film could have used it. The negative critical reception was fairly consistent, with most complaining of it feeling confused, undistinguished, and not gritty enough. In the end, the film is very watchable but fails because on the one hand, Silliphant didn't really crack the case in terms of adaptation, and Bogart's blandly workmanlike direction could have used more style. As a result, Philip Marlowe's gun ended H.M.'s decade not with a bang, but a whimper.

Chapter Twelve

The Utility Actor, Part 1 (1970-1971)

On-screen chemistry with Doris Day...
... and a life-changing off-screen affair.

*"I enjoyed the '70's very much. It was a very good time
in my life. I knew who I was and what I was doing."*

TV dramas from the 1950's often focused on a central character fighting/solving crimes (*Peter Gunn, Perry Mason, The Untouchables, The Rifleman*). By comparison, the 1960's was often an experimental free-for-all in terms of the weekly protagonist. As detailed in the previous chapters, most hit shows of the sixties developed an ensemble cast or duo, whether Western (*Gunsmoke, Bonanza, The Big Valley, The Wild, Wild West*) or Crime show (*Mission: Impossible, I Spy, The Man from U.N.C.L.E.*). In some episodes from the 1960's, the main cast would practically recede and become supporting players, as in H.M.'s episode of *The Virginian* with fellow guest star, Ricardo Montalban (discussed in the previous chapter), which provided meaty roles only to the week's three or four guest stars. When one combines this with how many anthology shows were on the air in the 1950's and 1960's, with rotating casts (*The Twilight Zone, The Outer Limits, Alfred Hitchcock Presents, Thriller, Playhouse 90, The Loretta Young Show,* et al), it was clear how actors like H.M. could find gratifying lead roles without having to be a series regular.

Perhaps it was the success of *Ironside* (which premiered in 1967 and ran until 1975) that brought back the singular, crime-solving/fighting hero (cop/detective/PI/lawyer) in a show that sported his last name as the series title. The use of "his" is deliberate as one is hard-pressed to find a crime-fighting/solving female in the lot, save for *Police Woman* and *Get Christie Love!* As for the extinction of the anthology show by the 1970's, it was likely an evolutionary combination of being more expensive to produce and audiences gravitating towards consistent casts in which they could become emotionally invested.

The 1970's brought every sort of ethnically ambiguous surname television linguists could come up with: *Kojak, Mannix, Cannon, Baretta, The Rockford Files*, et al. And unlike the 1960's, that star was expected to carry the episode each week, often appearing in nearly every scene. There would be a guest villain each episode which would be the plum role (*Columbo* certainly mastered this). But if an actor wasn't cast as THE villain guest star, the role was usually tailored for a utility actor, i.e., someone dependable who could put on a uniform and play "the major" for two scenes or don a suit to play "warden" or "FBI agent" for three scenes. It provided steady work and income, but usually little challenge in terms of acting.

Therefore, it's interesting that H.M. remembers the 1970's so fondly in terms of career. He was certainly working steadily on a variety of hit shows — which was always his objective — but it is difficult to point to many roles that were as rich or nuanced as those detailed in the last six chapters.

In 1970 alone, he was cast twice as "Colonels". In a Season Two episode of *The Name of the Game*, H.M. played Colonel Mara opposite his frequent *The Untouchables* co-star, Robert Stack, along with Gene Barry and Tony Franciosa. Soon after, he was cast as the gruff, annoyed Colonel Sindell in a two-part episode of *Hawaii Five-O*. In the latter, Ed Flanders had the key guest role: a brilliant scientist who once worked for the U.S. government but who now wants to expose the terrible things he was working on by releasing a deadly bacteria developed in the lab, which could result in millions of deaths. H.M. is in a number of scenes, but his prime direction is to be angry about what Flanders is up to.

H.M. did have some fun in 1970 as the guest villain on his second and final episode of *Get Smart*, directed by its star, Don Adams. Technically, series lead Barbara Feldon was the main villain, playing an imposter from enemy agency KAOS who pretends to be Smart's wife, Agent 99, in order to poison Smart and frame the real Agent 99 for murder. H.M. played Melnick Archer, the owner of Melnick's Furniture, a front for some of KAOS's nefarious deeds. In this case, Melnick is using his furniture warehouse to hold the real Agent 99 captive, and she is very impressed with the comfortable and stylish furniture in her prison cell.

But as the busier 1971 began, his first appearance on TV was in uniform as Captain Strom on *Mission: Impossible*, sporting the regimentals (and accent) of some unnamed enemy nation (hint: Russia) that is plotting to use their secret satellites to threaten the USA. H.M. is on screen quite a bit, always in the secret control

In a second episode of *Get Smart*, with the enemy organization logo emblazoned behind him.

room, working under General Marin (*The Night Stalker*'s Barry Atwater).

1971 also brought a glimpse into the romantic comedy chemistry that H.M. delivered when infrequently called upon to do so. It occurred opposite no less than the impeccable comedy gifts of screen legend, Doris Day, on the second of his two 1971 episodes of *The Doris Day Show*. His Season Three episode, broadcast in March, was a small role and beneath him, but his Season Four episode, "Mr. and Mrs. Raffles", which aired in September, offered audiences a glimpse into a new side of H.M.

As the bespectacled Captain Strom from the unnamed foreign power plotting to use secret satellites to threaten the U.S. on his fourth episode of *Mission: Impossible*. With Leonard Nimoy (seated).

In the episode, Day and her neighbor are mistaken for jewel thieves, and no matter how they try to rectify it, they get in deeper and deeper. This lands Day and her neighbor in a holding cell where Day is propositioned by an attractive jewel thief, Rodney (H.M.) to go into business together on a heist after they're released. She accepts, leading to a climactic heist during which we realize that Rodney is an undercover detective, using Day and her neighbor as bait to catch the real thieves. But it is that jail cell scene with Day that is the eye-opener. H.M. and Day have real, sexy, even dangerous chemistry, since H.M. is believed to be the bad boy.

Prison meet-cute with Doris Day. H.M. played an undercover cop masquerading as a jewel thief on *The Doris Day Show*.

"I loved working with her," H.M. remembered of Doris Day. "She knew how to make me feel instantly comfortable opposite her."

As with his two episodes of *The Loretta Young Show*, ten years earlier (also broadcast within the same year) it is a refreshing glimpse into the many sides of H.M., but also a bit frustrating as it makes one wish he had done far more light comedy and not been pigeon-holed as "The Heavy".

His Season Six episode that same year of *Hogan's Heroes* ("To Russia Without Love") managed to combine both of these

Hogan's Heroes - H.M.'s Nazi Colonel Becker will soon learn that it's never a good idea to double-cross Colonel Hogan (Bob Crane).

qualities: comedy and heavy. H.M. is the lead guest star, Nazi Colonel Becker, who is visiting from the undesirable prison camp he runs in frozen Siberia. Becker covets Colonel Klink's (Werner Klemperer) cushy gig and makes a deal with Hogan (Bob Crane) that if Hogan manipulates Klink into trading camps with Becker, he will go easy on the prisoners. Hogan and the boys deliver on the deal, making Klink believe Siberia is a sunny paradise with women galore. As the excited Klink is readying for his transfer, Becker shows his true tyrannical colors to Hogan, who essentially murders Becker for the betrayal, albeit off screen, and arranges it to look like he accidentally blew himself up. Clearly, Colonel Becker would not be coming back for future episodes.

"Werner Klemperer had the penthouse at the Sunset Tower. We played a lot of poker there," recalled H.M. with a smile.

More work came that year, such as a decent role on *Mannix* as a duplicitous cop partnered with the equally corrupt cop played by Robert Foxworth, who had the main guest villain role that week. Also, an episode of Burt Reynolds' one season ABC detective series, *Dan August* ("Burt was a good guy. He didn't play on being a star."), but it was in the little remembered, one-season Rod Taylor adventure series, *Bearcats!*, where the first hints that a seismic shift was about to come in H.M. Wynant's life.

Bruce, his youngest son, was just turning fourteen at the

time and was the only one of his three boys who wanted to be an actor. The oldest, Bill, was focused on music at Cal Arts (drumming specifically), and Scott was beginning his time at UCLA with his eye on a behind-the-scenes career in Television, producing and directing. Bruce would be the family member who ran lines with his father, helping him learn each new role that came week after week.

Occasionally, H.M. would have the eager teen join him on location, as he did in the summer of '71 when *Bearcats!* was shooting in Santa Fe, New Mexico. Bruce recalled having a wonderful time watching his father play the episode's big villain, an oil baron trying to frame the local Native Americans for sabotage. When H.M.'s character was supposed to shoot a flaming arrow, he told the director he could do it without the need of the stuntman. Unfortunately, the arrow set H.M.'s arm on fire and fell short of its mark, starting a fire on a derrick! Luckily, the fire was contained and the only injury H.M. sustained was a very bruised ego.

But there were other flames H.M. was stoking at that time, those of a serious affair with Cynthia Baer McMartin, who was at the end of her eleven-year marriage to stage and TV actor, John McMartin. Bruce recalled his father stepping outside to make phone calls every night when they were on location for *Bearcats!*. Curious, Bruce followed him one night and overheard his father whispering a lot of sweet nothings to someone on the other end of the payphone. He was certain his father was not talking to his mother, Ethel, because all three boys knew their parents' marriage was becoming equal parts distant and tense, with little, if any, romance.

The nightly clandestine phone calls from the set of *Bearcats!* led to H.M. abruptly sending Bruce back to LA early, which the boy came to realize was hastened because Cynthia was coming to the set for a visit.

Chapter Thirteen

The Utility Actor, Part 2 (1971-1973)

The Planet of the Apes Saga, Jean Renoir,
and the end of a marriage.

*"Communication between Ethel and I became nonexistent.
Less and less until there wasn't any."*

Cynthia Baer was four years younger than H.M., born in St. Paul, Minnesota, to a fairly well-to-do family. After a brief acting career (The Internet Movie Database lists three small roles on episodic TV from 1956 to 1957, all shot in New York), she turned to the theater, producing the New York premiere of *Little Mary Sunshine*, an Off-Broadway send-up of operettas that opened in late 1959 and had a nearly three-year run. Within a year of its closing, she wed one of its stars, John McMartin, a New York stage actor on the rise, who ultimately received five Tony Award nominations over the course of his career. The couple had two daughters, Kathleen and Susan, ages seven and three, respectively, at the time of *Bearcats!*.

The clandestine relationship continued a few more months as H.M. completed his eighth and final episode of *Gunsmoke* ("No Tomorrow") as Morris Gragin, a shady prosecutor, as well as the third and best of his *Hawaii Five-O* episodes, "While You're at It,

Bring in the Moon". It was an Agatha Christie type episode where an eccentric germaphobe millionaire (Barry Sullivan) was framed for the murder of one of his five key business partners. H.M. was one of the four suspects — the ladies' man of the bunch. The real killer turned out to be the business partner played by Ed Flanders who, coincidentally, was also H.M.'s costar in his 1970 *Hawaii Five-O* two-parter. Apparently, neither the network nor audiences seemed to care about such things. Of interest is that he was mistakenly billed in the credits as "H.M. Winant", a spelling he had changed 13 years earlier but which Ethel and the children main-

Embroiled in an Agatha Christie-esque episode of *Hawaii Five-O* with Jack Lord.

tained. Perhaps someone in CBS post-production assumed H.M. spelled it the same as their boss.

H.M. finally fessed-up to Ethel about the relationship with Cynthia and his belief that their 20-year marriage was over. After many fights and mutual tears, the couple gathered their three boys and broke the not-unexpected news to them. According to Bruce, "We all looked at them and said, 'Oh God, it's about time.'"

"What? We were staying together because of you three!" the couple replied to their boys, now ranging in age from 15 to 19.

Ethel had no patience for the situation, so when she told H.M. to leave the house immediately, he acquiesced, moving into a temporary apartment. Divorce proceedings began swiftly, which was difficult for all involved.

"I remember being on set for the first of three episodes I did of *Cannon* with Bill Conrad," recalled H.M. "The separation from Ethel was literally happening during the show. Bill saw what I was going through and helped me. He was very kind."

From there, H.M. shot his fourth and final episode of *Mission: Impossible* as incarcerated crime figure, Gunther Schell, described as "the brains behind the syndicate's illegal money operations". Schell falls victim to an escape scam wherein incarcerated crooks are seduced with freedom but instead are given a psychedelic truth serum to find out where they hid the stolen money. In

Schell's case, $27 million.

As word began to spread within the TV world of H.M.'s breakup with the most powerful female executive in Television, H.M. and his representation thought it wise to set their sights on features, leading to H.M. being cast as a part of yet another iconic piece of pop culture: the *Planet of the Apes* series.

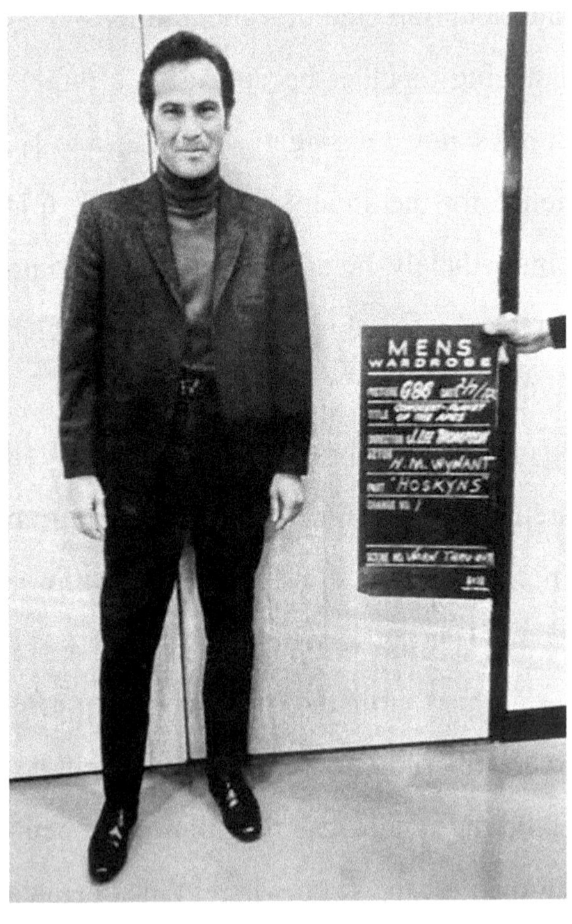

Rare wardrobe test photo for *Conquest of the Planet of the Apes* (1972). In the future of 1990, all men will wear dark sport coats and turtlenecks, especially the bad guys.

Conquest of the Planet of the Apes went into production on January 31, 1972. The fourth film in the series, it told the story of the thought-to-be-dead, intelligent, speaking-ape offspring of Cornelius and Zira, both of whom had been assassinated at the end of the prior film, *Escape from the Planet of the Apes* (1971). In the last act of *Escape*, set in the present of 1971, Zira had done a switcheroo with her newborn, Milo, and another newborn chimp in the circus of Armando (Ricardo Montalban).

Now it is 1991 and Armando is bringing young adult Milo (Roddy McDowall) to the big city to see the world. Unfortunately, when anger causes Milo to speak in public, they are forced to separate, leading to Armando's capture and interrogation by two government men in the employ of the charmingly vile Governor Breck (Don Murray, cast effectively against type). The duo are Kolp (Severn Darden) and Hoskyns (H.M.), both donning the grey turtlenecks and charcoal sport coats that were apparently all the rage in 1991 via 1972.

As H.M. recalled on the *Damn Dirty Geeks* podcast in 2017: "There were two of us up for the role. The other guy thought he got it. We were both part of a golf group called 'The Hollywood Hackers'. I can't remember his name. When I got it, he gave me bloody hell!"

"Severn Darden and I were the bad guys, and he really blew me away. You just look at him and he can't do anything wrong. His sound, the way he looks, is just so right for villains. He doesn't have to do anything but stand there and say the words."

When asked about Don Murray, with whom he had worked three years earlier on *The Outcasts*: "I got Don his first job! It was in New York, 1954 or '55. His father, Denny Murray, was the stage manager on *High Button Shoes*. I was the lead dancer on a New York TV show called *Ken Murray's Blackouts*. Don was two years younger than me and he wanted to get in the business. I said come with me, and got him on the show. It was before unions. He got ten bucks!"

Conquest was the fourth time H.M. worked with his old friend, Montalban, and this time he was responsible for Montalban's death after he cracks from the interrogation he is submitted to at the hands of Kolp and Hoskyns. "I felt bad about killing Ricardo. He was a friend!" H.M. said more recently with a chuckle.

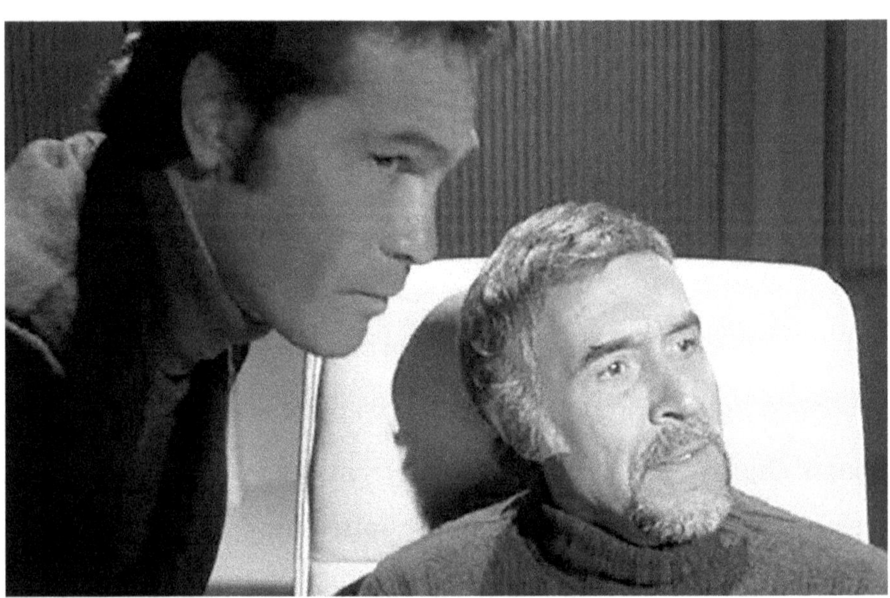

With old friend and frequent costar, Ricardo Montalban, just before the latter is driven to suicide by H.M. and his fellow tormentors in *Conquest of the Planet of the Apes.*

In the latter part of 1972, H.M. appeared in three important movies for television, one of which is an artistic high point for the medium and two of which are paranormal cult classics.

In May of 1970, Los Angeles' public broadcasting network, KCET, launched *Hollywood Television Theater*, a series of original, televised plays and classic dramas, utilizing the station's Hollywood connections to rein in all-star talent. The series' Emmy Award-winning premiere production was Saul Levitt's play, "The Anderson Trial", directed by George C. Scott and starred William Shatner, Martin Sheen, and Buddy Ebsen. Although not broadcast live, the shows were nevertheless blocked and shot with four cameras in large chunks and then edited together, giving them the feel of a *Playhouse 90* episode.

By 1972, actor/director/producer Norman Lloyd had gotten involved in the series and directed Clifford Odets' "Awake and Sing", starring Walter Matthau. Now one of the executive producers of the series, Lloyd discovered that his friend, the great French filmmaker Jean Renoir (with whom Lloyd had grown close after acting in Renoir's 1945 Hollywood film, *The Southerner*) had a stage play he was seeking to produce entitled, *Carola*. Lloyd convinced Renoir to allow the play to premiere as part of *Hollywood Television Theater*, with Renoir directing an English language translation by James Bridges, who had written a number of episodes of *Alfred Hitchcock Presents*, which Lloyd had produced (Bridges would go on to write and direct *The Paper Chase*, *The China Syndrome*, and *Urban Cowboy*). When 78-year-old Renoir became too ill to direct, he asked Lloyd to take the helm, which he was honored to accept.

Shot at the end of 1972 at KCET's new (at the time) studio space on Sunset Boulevard in Hollywood, it took place during World War II, mostly in the dressing room of a great French stage star named Carola Jannsen (Leslie Caron). Carola is informed by her Stage Manager, Campan (Anthony Zerbe) that German general Franz von Clodius (Mel Ferrer) would like to pay her a visit. The manipulative Campan wants Carola to allow Clodius' visit and be friendly, as it will allow the theater company to stay in the good graces of the Nazis and not be shut down. What Campan doesn't know is that Carola and Clodius have a romantic past.

As part of this remarkable cast, H.M. was cast as Camille, Assistant Stage Manager to Campan, who runs interference between Carola and the imminent arrival of Clodius. It was an apropos casting choice since H.M. had actually held that job on Broadway two decades earlier in productions involving theater greats Katharine Hepburn, Laurence Olivier, and Rex Harrison. Under Lloyd's direction, on a richly detailed set designed by Eugène Lourié (who had been the production designer on all of Renoir's classic French films of the 1930's), the cast performed impeccably with each role, large and small, having something of substance to contribute, a hallmark of Renoir's work. The end result is a moving television production worthy of rediscovery.

As for H.M., he recalled it being a special project and greatly admired Norman Lloyd and acting opposite Leslie Caron in all his scenes, "But the strangest things stick with you fifty years later. Like Leslie Caron's antique Ford — with a rumble seat! Two seats in the front and two uncovered in the rear. Gorgeous! I'll never forget that car."

Both of the two cult-status, paranormal Movies of the Week (MOW) that followed were shot at the end of 1972 and broadcast in February of '73 on rival networks. At CBS, he appeared as Frank Driscoll, one of the co-pilots in *The Horror at 37,000 Feet*. Combining the *Airport* all-star disaster genre with the supernatural, it had a great cast (William Shatner, Chuck Connors, Buddy Ebsen, Tammy Grimes) in a story of how druid stones in the plane's cargo hold begin to exert a supernatural hold over the passengers and crew. It was a nutty entertainment to be sure, but unfortunately, H.M.'s role as one of the co-pilots gave him little to do but sit at the wheel and maintain control of the plane while Chuck Connors got to leave the cockpit to interact with the rest of the cast.

At NBC, H.M. appeared in the *Twilight Zone*-ish MOW, *The Stranger*, produced by Bing Crosby Productions, about an astronaut (Glenn Corbett) who lands on Terra, Earth's doppelgänger, and is hunted as an alien. In a white smock the entire time, H.M. plays Eric Stoner but is essentially "Scientist #2" with Tim O'Connor's senior scientist getting most of the lines and H.M. getting beaten up by the astronaut.

Both of these network MOWs presented the sort of roles that were well-beneath H.M.'s status and talent, but necessary for him to accept at the time given the financial responsibilities he would be facing when his inevitable divorce was finalized.

In the first half of 1973, H.M. did two more shows for CBS, episodes of *Cannon* and *Mannix*. But after he and Cynthia officially got married in Las Vegas on August 13, 1973, H.M. would not be cast on another CBS show until after Ethel left for NBC in 1979.

Chapter Fourteen

THE RESUME SKIPS A YEAR (1973-1977)

In Italy for a year with his new family.
In Austria for two months with Shirley Jones.

"Ethel could make or break an actor's career."

At the time of their 1971 divorce, Ethel Winant was arguably at the pinnacle of her power. As Television's first female Vice President, she was responsible for assembling the iconic casts of all its hit shows (*Mary Tyler Moore*, *Bob Newhart*, and the many spinoffs, to name only a few), including the phenomenon that was *All in the Family*, which premiered on January 12, 1971, an extremely tense, nail-biting night in the Wynant/Winant household, as son Bruce recalled, with Ethel planted in front of the master bedroom's color TV, fielding calls on both of her two bedside phones. It became the season's highest rated series.

But after H.M. officially married Cynthia Baer in '73, he instantly seemed to become *persona non grata* at CBS. While there's no evidence that Ethel ever sent out a memo to that effect, no producer nor casting director would risk bringing H.M. into a casting discussion and for fear of upsetting their boss, Ethel.

And so, given the professional advice he was receiving to "lay low", coupled with an opportunity afforded to Cynthia's children to go to school for a year in Europe, H.M., Cynthia, and her two daughters (now nine and five years old) moved to Rome for a year.

"We moved into a 4-story apartment of Piazza del Popolo. We traded residences with someone from Rome who wanted to stay in Cynthia's home in Beverly Glen. We went for one year while the girls attended school."

At 46, it was H.M.'s first trip to Europe, let alone outside the U.S. He loved Italy. It was there he began to sculpt. "Richard Basehart and I were great friends, and his wife Diana was a sculptress. She gave Cynthia a tiny piece of stone to work on while she was in Italy and gave her a tool to work with to calm her nerves. She fussed and fussed with it and finally, I couldn't stand looking at it anymore, so I took it out of her hand and made something out of it, and that started me."[5]

He sent postcards to his boys but could not afford to fly them to Rome for a visit. By that point, Billy (age 20) and Scott (age 19) were at Cal Arts and USC, respectively. Only 16-year-old Bruce was living at home, with Ethel, who had regrettably sold the Westwood home under market price, against the advice of H.M. and everyone she knew, except for her business managers, who ultimately swindled her out of her money. "She had a great head

[5]The Encyclopedia of Hollywood, Vol. 3, by Tom & Jim Goldrup

for television and a terrible head for business," recalled Bruce, a sentiment echoed by H.M.

H.M. had been working non-stop since first setting foot on Broadway twenty-seven years earlier. In New York, he worked day *and* night, live TV in the day and arriving at the theater in time for the curtain to rise. Then, to Los Angeles for one show or movie after the other, always shooting in LA or locations somewhere in the US. That H.M. recalled the 1970's so fondly is further testament to his ability to live in the moment, day by day, and not be so driven by ambition, like most of his peers. He did miss the work, but he also found Rome invigorating and rejuvenating, enjoying his first real honeymoon as well as the simple pleasures of Italian foods, coffee, drives in the country, learning to sculpt, and being a full-time father to two daughters for the first time in his life. Accurate or not, he also felt confident that once the year was over, he would return to Los Angeles and pick up where he left off.

"I remember two things about my Dad's time in Rome," said Bruce. "He came back an amazing sculptor, and he had a Maserati."

As H.M. eleborated, "We put the Maserati on the ship with us, crossed the Atlantic, arrived in New York, and drove it across country back to LA. On hindsight, I felt bad for the girls since they had to both fit in the tiny back seat."

Upon returning to their home on Beverly Glen in the hills of Los Angeles in the latter part of 1974, H.M. set out to reestablish himself professionally. He had had no on-air credits in the entirety of 1974, but did find work at NBC on a Season Two episode of *The Rockford Files*, broadcast in '75, as the well-tailored muscle to a real estate villain who didn't like what Jim Rockford (James Garner) was sticking his nose into that week. A second NBC show, the legal drama, *Petrocelli*, followed, and two for ABC: the hit cop show, *S.W.A.T.*, and the sensation that was *The Six Million Dollar Man*, bringing his 1975 tally to four shows. Unfortunately, despite the marquee value, none of the roles were substantive nor memorable, but they were work.

The end of 1975 saw him add Elia Kazan to the list of genius directors for whom he worked. It was a memorable one-scene bit in Kazan's last studio movie, *The Last Tycoon*, written by Harold Pinter, starring Robert De Niro in F. Scott Fitzgerald's thinly veiled story of studio head, Irving Thalberg. Mike Fenton, who had cast H.M. in *I Spy*, was in charge of casting

"I was asked to do it, so I did it," H.M. recalled matter-of-factly. "I remember that it was very pleasant to be there and to do it. I loved Bob Mitchum."

After viewing a black-and-white, romantic farewell scene on-screen between Tony Curtis and Jeanne Moreau, the lights come up in silence in the studio screening room where all wait for Monroe Stahr's (Robert De Niro) opinion. There are 12 gathered, but only four engage in dialogue. Robert Mitchum (as the Chairman of the Board) is the first to break the ice, complimenting H.M. on "the French girls" ("Yes, I think they have depth," H.M.'s unnamed Associate Producer, a total suck-up, replies).

1976 saw him don a pilot's uniform and cap to show up in the last reel and save the day in the two-hour pilot for NBC's *The Gemini Man*. In a finale clearly inspired by *Airport '75*, H.M. followed Charlton Heston's playbook, manning the radio on the ground and guiding a non-pilot (an invisible one no less!) on how to land a jumbo jet. A nice role as a police lieutenant who has to

As a studio kiss-ass in a fun, one-scene bit in Elia Kazan's *The Last Tycoon*. Pictured with Robert Mitchum.

break bad news to Tony Lo Bianco came next on the Joseph Wambaugh-created *Police Story*, also on NBC.

The remainder of '76 and first half of '77 were busy. True, he had some lackluster roles in *Future Cop* with Ernest Borgnine, and a second *The Six Million Dollar Man*. But he did have a fun, red-herring role as a pesky journalist opposite his old *Teahouse of the August Moon* co-star David Wayne in *The Nancy Drew Mysteries*, shot entirely on the Queen Mary. He also had two good parts in episodes of *Quincy, M.E.* in both Seasons 1 and 2. In the first, "A Star is Dead", which has a genuinely shocking denouement, he played the campaign manager for a murder suspect, and congressional candidate, played by his one-time *Mannix* co-star, Robert Foxworth. Unfortunately, because Foxworth ends his campaign, H.M.'s character is missing from the last act fireworks. In the Season 2 episode, "Hit and Run at Danny's", he plays a bigwig from the FBI who swoops in to work with Quincy, arresting the real killer and having the cute closing scene with Jack Klugman's titular medical examiner. Both were solid, substantive guest roles, so it could only be poor representation that H.M. is credited in the "co-starring" tail credits for both episodes instead of the up-front "Guest Starring" roster, especially given the first episode has five Guest Stars and then Foxworth as "Special Guest Star"

But in early 1977, an opportunity presented itself unlike

anything he'd done since New York: live musical theater.

Cynthia had been immersed in the world of musical theater through her own producing career and that of her ex-husband, actor John McMartin. As a result, she had grown close with Shirley Jones who, at the time, was recently divorced from actor Jack Cassidy. H.M. and Cynthia spent time as a foursome with Shirley and Jack, a brilliant, charismatic, but deeply troubled man who suffered from both alcoholism and bipolar disorder.

"I liked Jack. He had class," remembered H.M. "He had a wardrobe that was unbelievable. After he died, it was put up for

As Robert Foxworth's campaign manager who tried to outmaneuver star Jack Klugman in one of two episodes of *Quincy, M.E.*

auction. It was that impressive."

On the evening of December 11, 1976, Cassidy reached out to Shirley to rekindle the relationship. Even though he still had a great hold on her heart (as Shirley herself later admitted), she refused to go to him that night. In the early hours of December 12th, Cassidy's West Hollywood apartment went up in flames. Cassidy's charred remains were found and it was believed he had fallen asleep with a lit cigarette, which caused his naugahyde couch to catch fire. But H.M. questioned that assessment.

"The talk was that someone killed him," H.M. remembered. "I don't believe he accidentally took his own life. None of us did. He had lots of enemies. Lots. Social enemies. He had boyfriends, girlfriends."

During the period between Cassidy and husband-to-be, comedian Mary Ingels, Shirley became "drinking buddies" with Cynthia, according to H.M. There was also an attraction of sorts within this trio: Shirley, Cynthia, and H.M. One day, Shirley impulsively suggested that she, Cynthia, and H.M. drive out to the Madonna Inn in San Luis Obispo, California, and get a room with one bed.

"I slept in the middle," H.M. explained. "It was love without sex. No touching. I slept in between the two ladies."

Early in 1977, in an effort to distance herself from the tragedy of her ex-husband, Shirley, 42 years old at the time, accepted an offer to star as Maria in a national tour of *The Sound of Music*, to commence that summer. It was Cynthia who insisted that H.M. should be Shirley's Captain Von Trapp. Shirley agreed, which could not have made H.M. happier, as he had always found the stage more satisfying and invigorating than either Television or Film acting.

At age 50, it would be his first lead in a first-class production of a Broadway musical. But it almost didn't happen.

"A couple of months before the first rehearsal, I was with Shirley at an old folks home trying out the song, 'Edelweiss'. Halfway through, I couldn't hear the end of the song. I finished, I went to the wings, and I collapsed. I'd had a brain aneurysm. The next thing I knew, I woke up in Century City Hospital. They drained my spine of blood. I was in Intensive Care for three weeks. Then, they put me in a room and I recovered. Shirley came to my room with my guitar and said, 'Do you still want to do it? We go into rehearsals in less than six weeks.' The doctor said no, but I said yes."

With Broadway's James M. Nederlander as one of its producers, H.M. and Shirley opened the national tour of *The Sound of Music* on June 28, 1977 at the Music Hall at Fair Park in Dallas, which seated over 3000 people. It was a six-city, ten-week tour, playing massive live theaters, and filling them every night.

Playing the Captain Von Trapp in the national tour of *The Sound of Music* opposite dear friend, Shirley Jones, as Maria.

"For half the run in Dallas, I had multiple vision. But then one morning, I woke up in the hotel, went to the balcony, and everything was single. My vision had come back overnight."

H.M. now admitted that the situation between he and Shirley became intimate on the road. "It was a hotel on the water. Mi-

The third Van Trapp child from right, Brigitta, was played by Sarah Jessica Parker.

Here, Sarah is the second child from the right.

ami, I believe. We had a relationship. It was a normal thing when you're on the road. We were a couple, but separately. And then, when we came back home, it was just understood that it was over."

Also of note is that the role of one of his daughters, Brigitta Von Trapp, was played by 12-year-old Sarah Jessica Parker, who would of course go on to fame headlining the HBO series, *Sex and the City*.

"I bumped into Sarah years later, after *Sex and the City*, at Musso and Frank in Hollywood. She got up from the opposite end of the restaurant and yelled, 'Poppa!'"

Thinking back on it, H.M. stated definitively, "I enjoyed that role more than anything I've ever done."

Chapter Fifteen

THE MUSTACHE EMERGES (1978-1984)

Bigfoot, Jesus, and J.R. Ewing

"To this day, I can quote entire scenes from the theater but not a word from any movie or TV show I ever did."

The mustache H.M. had grown to play Captain Von Trapp remained a permanent fixture upon returning to Los Angeles. Although it made him look even more like Burt Reynolds, perhaps it felt like a fresh coat of paint since TV and Film roles were not as exciting in the run-up to *The Sound of Music* tour.

Despite the several-months break to rehearse and perform the musical in six cities, he returned to work immediately with a two-parter of *Police Story* on NBC. Unfortunately, the plum guest roles in that episode went to Steve Lawrence, Claude Akins, and Warren Stevens, with reliable H.M. playing "the Warden" for just one scene (albeit an intense one) opposite Akins, who played an incarcerated cop.

The pilot for 1978's *Sword of Justice* came next, playing all his scenes with Larry Hagman, and then on to NBC's short-lived, proto-*21 Jump Street* cop show, *David Cassidy: Man Under Cover*, in a one-scene bit, again, as "the Warden", the second time that year.

Of troubled young pop star, David Cassidy, H.M. recalled, "David was very arrogant, both on set and in life. To my eyes, his relationship with Shirley (his stepmother) seemed non-existent. Despite doing *The Partridge Family* together, I don't think they spoke much to each other."

H.M. further elaborated on the topic of nepotism, "The last name gives them stature and they either ignore it or live it. I think you should ignore it and be your own person, but some - like David - accept it and trade on it, even though they don't deserve it."

The year also saw H.M. take a trip down memory lane when veteran writer/creator Merwin Gerard managed to relaunch his pre-*The Twilight Zone* supernatural anthology series *Once Step Beyond* (which had run for three seasons, from 1959 to 1961), now rechristened *The Next Step Beyond*. Nearly twenty years older, original host, John Newland, once again stepped into frame and introduced each episode, now sporting a white mane of hair and thick-framed glasses. As with the previous series, Newland also directed most of the episodes. H.M. had appeared on two of the better episodes of the earlier series (see Chapters Seven and Eight) and here co-starred in the episode, "Other Voices". Thankfully, it was a substantive role as Frank, a violent, abusive husband seen in a premonition by episode protagonist, Walter (Robert Walker Jr.), who believes Frank is going to kill his wife. Unfortunately,

Walter's premonition of Frank's violence proves accurate, except it's Walter himself who Frank murders.

Unfortunately, the low budget, shot-on-videotape reboot (many of the scripts were purportedly ill-disguised retreads of old episodes with some name changes) did not manage to inspire either critics or viewers and so the show lasted only one, 25-episode season.

1978 also brought about H.M.'s involvement with the infamous Sunn Classic Pictures. Also known as Schick-Sunn Classics and, briefly, Taft International Pictures, it was founded in 1971 in Park City, Utah, by Raylon Jensen with the help of the Schick Razor Company. To compete, they would research underserved markets, pay to book their movies into theaters (called "four-walling") for two weeks, advertise a "one week only" engagement, then miraculously announce "Held over one more week!"

Their biggest hit was 1974's *The Life and Times of Grizzly Adams*, leading to three sequels and a hit TV series. H.M.'s first production for them was their "documentary", *In Search of Historic Jesus* (released in 1979). Why the use of sarcasm quotes? Consider this: the Narrator asks, "Was there really a "Star of Bethlehem? To find out, we came here, to talk to Dr. Robert McClain in his observatory." The Dr. McClaim who explains to us the likelihood that it was, in fact, a miraculous occurrence is none other than H.M. This "documentary" doesn't even attempt to conceal the falsehood, listing H.M. in the final credit roll as having played "The Astronomer". Despite blatant hucksterism and terrible reviews, the film went on to box office success.

That same year, Sunn Classics made a deal with NBC for a series called *Greatest Heroes of the Bible*. Shot in Paige, Arizona, H.M (with a real mustache and fake beard) appeared in the second episode, "Samson and Delilah", as the influential leader of the City Elders who pesters the Governor (James Olson) to do something about Samson (John Beck). In the climax, H.M. is one of the key enemies of Samson who gets pummeled by Styrofoam columns.

The year that followed, 1979, may have been H.M.'s nadir in terms of the quality of the roles and the credibility it afforded him as an actor. Along with the release that year of the aforementioned *In Search of Historic Jesus*, he appeared in NBC's disastrously miscalculated event series premiere, *Supertrain*. Produced and directed by *Dark Shadows'* Dan Curtis, the series attempted to put a quasi-*Love Boat/Fantasy Island* onboard a high-tech, futuristic, cross-country, luxury train: multiple parallel stories each week with a celebrity cast. Despite the first episode having Steve Lawrence, Keenan Wynn, Fred Williamson, and George Hamilton, H.M.'s character never even stepped on the train, playing one of the members of the board who reluctantly approved the expensive train's maiden voyage in the episode's earliest scenes.

The series was very expensive, went overbudget, and ultimately received deservedly terrible reviews and ratings. The producers tried desperate measures to win audiences by shifting into comedy, even adding a laugh-track, a la *The Love Boat*. This was indeed an odd choice given that the pilot episode was titled "Express to Terror". It didn't help with critics nor audiences and the show was cancelled. But the larger point here, in terms of H.M., is that it was a role he should never have accepted but was finding put before him more and more by his less-than-esteemed representation at the time.

The program in which H.M. appeared that is perhaps most suitable for a *Mystery Science Theater* presentation (if they were to serve up a TV show rather than movie) would have to be his episode of 1979's Syd and Marty Krofft Saturday morning show, *Bigfoot and Wildboy*. In the episode ("The Secret Invasion"), series regular Cindy (Yvonne Regalado) is on an expedition with her archeology teacher, Professor Sewell (H.M.), only to discover the cave-dwelling Lohr-Khan tribe, who plan to contaminate the water supply and conquer the world. In order for Sewell to aid their nefarious agenda, the tribe turns him into a zombie with no will of his own until the titular leads arrive and duke it out with the cave dwellers, saving Cindy and the professor.

It is of note that the Lohr-Khan tribe dwell in the famed Bronson Caves, located in Hollywood at the edge of Griffith Park. Movie and TV fans know it well as the site of much iconic entertainment since the dawn of cinema, including TV's Bat Cave, John Ford's *The Searchers*, and sci-fi B movie cult classic *Robot Monster* to name only a few of the many hundreds of movies and TV shows filmed there.

With the 1970's concluding on such a low in terms of reputable projects, and with no TV credits in 1980, the eighties were not looking promising for H.M. in terms of career. Could things pick up in the new decade?

1980's Roswell-inspired UFO sci-fi thriller, *Hangar 18*, gave H.M. front billing (along with Darren McGavin, Robert Vaughn, and Gary Collins), which would imply a large role, but he only appeared on screen for an untaxing one-scene bit, ultimately billed as "Flight Director" in the tail credits. It was his second theatrical feature for Sunn Classics. A third and final feature for Sunn Classics in 1981, the financially unsuccessful sci-fi alien comedy, *Earthbound*, featured H.M. in an even less distinguished role.

Fortunately, things picked up in 1981 with a good part as a nattily dressed, cool-tempered, smooth as silk gangster opposite his old friend, William Conrad, in his post-*Cannon* series for NBC, *Nero Wolfe*.

Since Ethel had departed CBS in 1979 for NBC, the 1981-82 season saw H.M. back on CBS for the first time in almost ten years on the Number One show on TV, *Dallas*. H.M. played Ed Chapman, a New York literary agent working with series regular, Donna (Susan Howard) on a memoir about her family history that just might implicate the Ewing family, particularly patriarch, J.R. Ewing (Larry Hagman). While it was certainly a high-profile job, the three episodes gave H.M. little to do of substance, appearing in only one or two scenes per episode as a calming, supportive presence for the conflicted Donna. The next year, he would appear in another hit CBS show, *Falcon Crest*, but in an even less conse-

As literary agent, Ed Chapman, in three episodes of *Dallas*.

quential role, that of a generic, suited detective at a crime scene that could have been played by anyone. Regardless, for H.M., particularly at this time, all work was welcomed and accepted.

With H.M. now firmly embraced by NBC, Ethel's arrival there didn't seem to affect H.M.'s continuing employment at the network. In *Days of Our Lives*, his first daytime soap since 1965's *The Young Married*s, H.M. was hired to play Orby "Jens" Jensen, the mean, estranged father of three of the younger series regulars. Orby gets mixed up in the lives of his children only to engage in criminal activities with their friends and acquaintances, like drug smuggling and gun running. He ultimately appeared as Orby for thirteen episodes over three seasons, from 1982 to 1984.

"I knew it was a character that would have a beginning and end. I knew that up front." elaborated H.M. "I enjoyed the grind. It was fun. And it was a group of very good people. There's great atmosphere on a soap. It was like family. An intimate family. That's the good thing: you're playing family and you become family... I would walk down the street and people would call me by my character name. Everyone seemed to watch it."

On a personal front, H.M. had grown close with Richard Basehart. A celebrated actor who, like H.M., got his start on the Broadway stage, he came to Hollywood and established his reputation in Film Noirs of the 1950s, with leads in *He Walked By*

Night, *Tension*, and *The House on Telegraph Hill*. He went on to star in John Huston's *Moby Dick* as young Ishmael as well as in Fellini's *La Strada* as the acrobat and clown known as "The Fool". He would ultimately headline in the TV series, *Voyage to the Bottom of the Sea* for four seasons (1964-1968).

Although Basehart was thirteen years older than H.M., the two actors ran in similar circles for nearly three decades, both appearing on different episodes of *Playhouse 90* and *The Twilight Zone*. But it was the camaraderie between their respective wives, Cynthia and Diana, that brought the two men together in friendship.

In the early 1980's, Basehart spearheaded an attempt to foster live theater among his Los Angeles acting friends. As H.M. told the Los Angeles Times in January, 1988, "Richard always wanted a place on the West Coast for actors and directors to meet and flourish creatively and produce a wide variety of productions encompassing the classics as well as new works."

With the help of H.M. and their wives, Basehart created a small club of actors who would have play readings in Basehart's home. In early 1984, the group staged its first production in Hollywood, *Don Juan in Hell*, starring Basehart and H.M. Then, in 1984, shortly after Basehart had narrated a poem during the extinguishing of the flame at the closing ceremonies of the Summer

Olympics on August 12, 1984, he suffered a series of strokes.

"I spent every day with Richard in the hospital. He was miserable, so I got him all dressed up — nobody noticed — got him into a cab, and took him to Musso and Frank for dinner. Then, I got him back to his room and there was a homeless person eating his food! I got him back in bed and he died in the next day or two."

The death of Richard Basehart at age 70 on September 17, 1984 would change the course of H.M.'s life forever.

Chapter Sixteen

THE PLAYHOUSE & THE DOGHOUSE (1984-1989)

Building his first theater. Ending his second marriage.

"I always wanted to build a theater.
Theater is what interests me, not Film."

In 1984, at age 57, H.M. Wynant's Film and Television career was cooling off significantly. His last five episodes of *Days of Our Lives* as Orby Jensen were his only TV credits that year. From 1985 to 1987, he appeared on only three TV shows, one each year (*Airwolf* in '85, *Simon & Simon* in '86, and a second *Airwolf* in '87).

To keep his sanity in his downtime, he continued to embrace sculpting in the lovely backyard of the home he shared with Cynthia and the girls, both now in high school.

"The sculptures had become bigger and better. I worked in marble and my sculptures were sort of realistic, religious art. Why? I don't know because I'm not religious at all. My sculptures were thematic, usually more than one figure, and based on religion and figures in the Bible."[6]

He also had time for more theater, performing in *Fatty*, about tragic silent comedian Fatty Arbuckle, at the Tiffany Theater on the Sunset Strip in 1985. However, continuing Richard Basehart's legacy of professional-calibre, live, small theater in Los Angeles was something H.M., Cynthia, and Diana Basehart decided to continue after the actor's death. It was a welcome activity for H.M. and Cynthia to share, given that the tension in their marriage was beginning to escalate.

"She called all the shots. It was her house. She was something of a school marm with me." Cynthia also set down boundaries that upset H.M. with regards to her two daughters, as he explained, "I always felt like a 'Dutch Uncle' with the girls. Cynthia was very adamant in letting me know I was not their father."

With series star, Jan-Michael Vincent in *Airwolf*.

They called their new endeavor The Richard Basehart Theater Club, and for two years, had its moveable headquarters at the Jockey Club in Marina del Rey, then the West End Playhouse in Van Nuys, and finally Hollywood's Chamber Theater, where it staged short Chekhov farces as part of the Hollywood Fringe Festival.

But Diana, who came from money, always had a permanent theater as her goal. They were not only aided by actors of Basehart's and H.M.'s generation, but by young actors, too. Even H.M's youngest son, Bruce, got involved in the workshops and productions.

In early 1986, a 29-year-old actress named Paula Davis was referred to the Basehart Theater Club by her acting teacher, Arthur Mendoza, who taught classes out of his own 47-seat Actors Circle Theater, on Santa Monica Boulevard in West Hollywood. Paula reached out and became a member. One of her first interactions was to stop by H.M. and Cynthia's home in Beverly Glen to pick up a script. Cynthia greeted her and directed her to get the script from H.M., who was in the garage tinkering.

"My God, you've got blue eyes!" Paula remembered H.M. declaring upon first seeing her. To her mind, the meaning was clear, he was interested in her as more than just an actress.

Sporting a UK passport but raised in Detroit, Paula had

moved to Los Angeles with her then-husband, Ron, both of whom wanted to be actors. Due to personality clashes, it was a marriage that was essentially over by the time Paula entered the orbit of H.M. and the Basehart Theater Club.

Paula continued to participate in the Basehart's workshops, very conscious that there was a flirtation going on between her and H.M. At one point, Cynthia was directing Paula and H.M. in a workshop scene from James Goldman's *The Lion in Winter*, with H.M. as King Henry and Paula playing his young mistress, Alais. When the scene pivoted to physical romance, Paula became self-conscious, stiffening a bit due to the genuine heat that had developed between them. But it was Cynthia who urged them on.

"Oh no, no, no, darling! You must let him kiss you!" Cynthia insisted.

Paula complied.

Finally, on Labor Day weekend of 1986, H.M. found himself alone in Los Angeles. His oldest stepdaughter, Kathleen, was away while Cynthia had traveled out of state to look at colleges with the younger Susan. It was on that weekend that H.M. and Paula finally acted on their building flirtation.

As the passionate affair wore on for months, Paula grew increasingly dissatisfied with solely being H.M.'s mistress. Finally, after roughly a year, she told him in 1987, "You really need to be with someone else because I don't like this role."

H.M. voiced to Paula his unhappiness in his marriage but was not prepared — mentally or otherwise — for a second divorce. He and Cynthia had too much co-mingled, not the least of which was their partnership in building the permanent home of the Basehart Players at what would be christened, The Richard Basehart Playhouse in Woodland Hills.

Throughout 1987, H.M. and Paula would break up and then clandestinely reunite. All the while, H.M. was literally building The Richard Basehart Playhouse from the ground up with his own two hands, particularly in the latter half of the year.

"I designed and built it. I always wanted to build a theater. Theater is what interests me, not Film. It had been a warehouse. A huge empty space. Four walls. High ceiling. Perfect. There was no space for a control room, so I built a huge platform for it above the audience."

The 91-seat, Equity-waiver theater opened on January 8, 1988 with Los Angeles Mayor Tom Bradley in attendance. Also showing up that night was H.M.'s first wife, Ethel Winant, who after fifteen years, chose to take the high road and support their efforts. It would be the only time his ex-wife, current wife, and future wife would occupy the same space at the same time.

Their first production was a revival of the musical Cynthia

had produced in New York back in 1959, *Little Mary Sunshine*, now directed by Cynthia. Neither H.M. nor Paula were in the cast. Cynthia was the theater's President and Artistic Director while H.M. took the moniker of Executive Vice President and Managing Director.

"By making Cynthia President, you get her to do a lot of shit. The details shit. I didn't have time and couldn't care less," explained H.M. In terms of who actually paid for the theater, H.M. admitted, "Diana (Basehart) was the money bags. She paid for the theater, she and her mother. I had no money!"

As journalist Kirk Ellis reported in the Los Angeles Times on opening day:

Formerly a machine shop, the playhouse took its present shape in a scant 2 1/2 months--a feat that all involved are quick to credit to the round-the-clock efforts of H.M. Wynant. Diana Basehart said the place was "a hideous warehouse," with an inch-deep layer of grease on what would become the auditorium floor.

Wynant oversaw transformation of the 4,000-square-foot space, which now boasts a huge stage, a state-of-the-art lighting system and a posh lobby that doubles as an art gallery. The gallery is managed by

Diana Basehart, a sculptor, and features paintings by Cornish artist Fred Yates.

There were rough spots, however. Obtaining the required permits was difficult, construction of wheelchair access ramps led to a $35,000 cost overrun, and Wynant concedes to having made "unfortunate oversights" in the overall design. "If you sit in the seventh row, you're in trouble," he said jokingly.

Later in the article, Ellis added,

All 80 full-time members are "professional" actors —people with an established body of work who make their living acting. Angie Dickinson, Mickey Rooney, Shirley Jones, Mel Torme, Lee Meriwether and director Don Taylor are among the charter members.

In fact, actor-turned-director Don Taylor was the director of H.M.'s only credit for 1988 — the CBS TV Movie, *The Diamond Trap*, starring Howard Hessman and Brooke Shields. H.M. played a New York detective named Idrissi, a wisecracking member of Hessman's unit. It was a fairly forgettable MOW, unclear in its tone (family friendly comedy or gritty cop thriller?), and uneasily substituting downtown Los Angeles for Manhattan.

As the fall approached, H.M. had finally realized that he

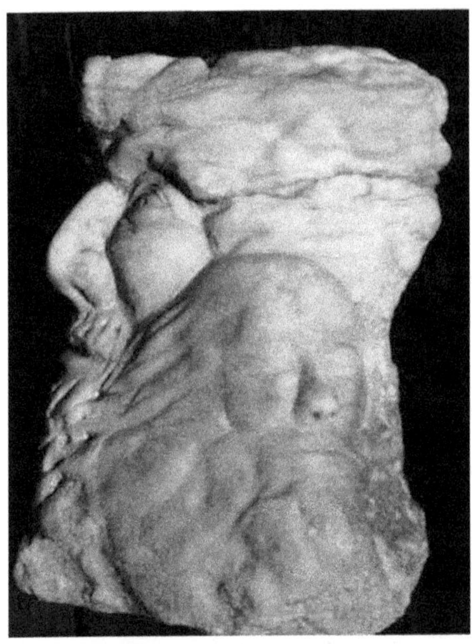

Chiselled by H.M. in Italian marble, this and one other work is all that remains of H.M.'s sculptures.

and Paula (now two years into their on-again/off-again relationship) were not just "a fling" and that something had to be done. He wanted to leave Cynthia and be with Paula. H.M. bit the bullet and spoke to the already-suspicious Cynthia about the relationship with Paula around the time of son Bruce's wedding on October 23, 1988. Within days of the wedding, Cynthia threw him out of their home on Beverly Glen. H.M and Paula agreed it would not be a good idea for him to move in with Paula (who by now was fully divorced from Ron and living alone) until his divorce was final. Instead, H.M. moved into a temporary furnished space at the Oakwood

Apartments on Barham Blvd in Toluca Lake.

It was an ugly breakup. Cynthia destroyed nearly all of H.M.'s memorabilia from his lifetime in the Theater, Film, and TV and left hostile messages on Paula's answering machine. And something even worse — she smashed to bits all of the sculptures H.M. had created. Sadly, H.M. would no longer have contact with Cynthia's daughters, but years later, the younger of the two would publish a short memoir of being a teenage girl dealing with her mother's alcoholism. H.M. does not recall thinking of Cynthia as an addict, but it is possible that her alcoholism may have contributed to how she handled the breakup. H.M. wanted to be done with the painful situation so he acquiesced on every point during the divorce proceedings, to his financial detriment.

Finally, on December 22, 1989, after sixteen years of marriage, H.M.'s second divorce was made final.

Chapter Seventeen

CHANGES GALORE (1990-2000)

Euro Disney, a third marriage, and a baby girl

"You do something, you're totally involved, but when it's over, the curtain is down. It's totally over. And you move on."

As 1990 began, H.M. and Paula moved into a rented house in West Hills, not far from the theater. Unfortunately, the divorce settlement stipulated that H.M. would no longer have any association with the Richard Basehart Playhouse, which stung H.M. deeply.

The blow was cushioned when H.M. was cast in one of the largest Guest Star roles of his career in ABC's Western series, *The*

Reunited with his siblings in Detroit, circa 1990, From left: Max, Charlie, Mollie.

Young Riders, which launched the careers of young series regulars, Josh Brolin, Chris Penn, and Stephen Baldwin. In the episode "Matched Pair", H.M. played Judge Enright, a corrupt land baron who used a gift of a matching pair of silver revolvers to seduce Brolin and Penn into his nefarious service. It was H.M.'s first Western series since his final appearance on *Gunsmoke* in 1972, eighteen years earlier.

H.M. also appeared in the most expensive movie of his career that year, the $43-million *Solar Crisis*. A Japanese-American independent coproduction, it was based on a Japanese novel involving a solar flare that threatens the earth. Tim Matheson played

H.M. as a corrupt land baron, handing the titular "Matched Pair" of guns to the impressionable Chris Penn and Josh Brolin in ABC's *The Young Riders*.

a military man dispatched to lead a mission to solve the problem. The film had a major pedigree, beginning with its all-star cast, including Charlton Heston as Matheson's father, Peter Boyle as the doubting IXL corporate bigwig, and Jack Palance as an eccentric loner who aids Matheson's son when the young man crashes in the desert. H.M. appeared early on as an unnamed IXL executive in a big meeting with Boyle.

The special effects were by two-time Oscar-winner, Richard Edlund (who was also a Producer on the film) of *Star Wars* fame, the music by three-time Oscar winner, Maurice Jarre (*Lawrence of Arabia*), and cinematography by Russell Carpenter who would go on to win an Oscar for *Titanic*. Directed by Richard C. Sarafian (*The Vanishing Point*), a good director, but a very odd choice for a $43 million, effects-laden space opera, it met with bad reviews and low attendance in its Japanese premiere. Expensive reshoots were done to secure a US distributor (Trimark) but the new cut did little to change the critical or audience reception. Displeased with the post-production process, Sarafian took his name off the film and utilized the DGA-sanctioned alias of Alan Smithee on the finished film.

Interestingly, H.M. shares all his time on-screen only with actor Paul Carr as a fellow IXL executive, serving up both story exposition and the details of the dramatic stakes. They appear together in a big boardroom scene with Peter Boyle, but are not seen in the wide shots nor with any other characters. Although H.M. cannot recall, it is likely H.M. and his off-screen friend, Paul Carr, were part of the Los Angeles reshoots to add hoped-for story clarity.

Despite divorcing Cynthia and renting a home with Paula, H.M. was still resistant to marrying a third time. In late '91, H.M.'s agent approached him with an opportunity at Disney. Apparently, no one was left at the company who remembered that H.M. had been fired over a morals clause for fooling around with an executive's girlfriend back in 1958, but the offer was not for a Disney movie. It was to be Buffalo Bill, starring in his own Wild West Show for soon-to-open Euro Disney in France. He interviewed along with several other candidates, but H.M. hit all the authenticity checkboxes: an actor with a long track record in

As Buffalo Bill, the star of Euro Disney's inaugural *Buffalo Bill's Wild West Show.*

Film and TV Westerns, an expert horseman, and a willingness to sign a one-year contract.

And so, in January of 1992, H.M. packed up and moved into an apartment in a town called Meaux, just east of Paris, close to Euro Disney, prepping for the high profile April opening of the new theme park.

H.M. enjoyed the character, the audiences, and grew very close with Peter MacLean, the other American actor playing Buffalo Bill on days when H.M. was off. Nine years younger than H.M., MacLean was also a TV veteran, but without the sort of iconic credits in H.M.'s resume. His most notable feature credits were decent roles in *The Friends of Eddie Coyle* (1973) with Robert Mitchum and the killer worm cult horror film, *Squirm* (1976).

H.M. also grew very close with his horse in the show, as he always has grown when assigned a horse for a production. But here, the assignment wasn't for days or weeks; it was for an entire year, so the bond was that much stronger. This created friction with the French trainer in charge of all the horses for the Wild West Show, including H.M.'s.

"He was incredibly arrogant and had no interest in anything I had to say," H.M. remembered, still bristling. "He killed so much of the joy of doing the show. When they asked for a second year renewal, I'd had enough, mostly because I couldn't stand having

Getting married to Paula in Malibu. Sister Mollie (pictured) flew in.

to work every day with that trainer. He was awful! I didn't like him and he didn't like me."

Paula joined him in France in the Spring for about six weeks, making a few appearances in the Wild West Show as the saloon girl who brings out the tray of champagne at the end. She also brought their cat, Mollie, to keep H.M. company for the rest of his stay. Ultimately, when the time came to renew his contract, H.M. decided he was ready to go home. MacLean took over as the main attraction Buffalo Bill for another four years.

When H.M. returned to California in January '93, he and Paula were in wedding preparation mode. It was a Roaring Twenties theme, combining ceremony and party at Monroe's in Malibu's Point Dume (now The Sunset Restaurant) with approximately sixty guests, including Ethel. A rabbi presided. Despite two previous marriages, it was H.M.'s first real wedding ceremony in front of family and friends. Ethel and Cynthia were both quickie ceremonies to "make it official", the first in a basement in Manhattan, the other in Las Vegas.

Shortly after, H.M. had a guest spot on the Steven Spielberg produced *SeaQuest 2032* (known in syndication as *SeaQuest DSV*) as one of the eight leaders of the UEO (United Earth Oceans organization). During a meeting on board Captain Roy Scheider's undersea vessel, all eight leaders seem to vanish, along with teenage series regular, Lucas (Jonathan Brandis). In reality, the meeting room was dropped several hundred feet and replaced with a doppelgänger room. It's all part of a dastardly power play to replace the UEO. Fortunately, Lucas manages to send out a signal. As the baddies try to fill the room with ocean water to drown all the leaders, Scheider arrives just in time to save the day.

The program would air in March of '94, just a month before the couple bought their first home together in Valley Glen, where they still reside as of this writing. And as this is just a short time before the author met H.M., it requires me to shift to first-person for a brief spell.

To backtrack for a moment, in 1992, a staged reading of my original, full-length play, *Karlaboy*, directed by Dennis Bartok (a best friend since attending NYU together, who would go on to direct the horror film, *Nails*) was mounted at the Hollywood Roosevelt Hotel. It drummed up interest from Jennifer Taylor Scott, who was running Arthur Mendoza's Actors Circle Theater. After Dennis had moved on to other things, I decided to direct the premiere myself, raised the money, secured the partnership of Actors Circle Theater, and began casting.

In the play, Bill, a biographer, has penned a ruthless tell-all about 1950's movie legend Karla Daven, a long-dead, legendary starlet. Bill is summoned in the middle of the night to the dilapidated mansion of her celebrity husband, Harold Bachman, a reclusive director. Harold swears that Karla's ghost has threatened to kill the director this night unless Bill calls off the book's publication. What follows is an intense evening where memory wrestles with myth to find the truth. As Harold gets deeper into exposing Bill's lies about Karla, he is forced to confront the

Publicity photo for H.M.'s starring role in the stage play, *Karlaboy*. James McManus (left), Ellie Valleau (right).

lies he's told himself – lies about himself as a filmmaker, a husband, and as a man. Harold must not only save himself from Karla's ghost, but from the ghosts of an unrealized life.

The play is split between real-time scenes in the present between Harold and Bill and flashbacks to Harold's life in the 1950's with Karla. Structurally influenced by Peter Schaffer's stage play, *Amadeus*, the intention was to cast one actor as both old Harold and young Harold, with the effect that we're never seeing pure flashback, but rather, something viewed through unreliable recollection. Try as we might, we could not find an actor who could play both old Harold and young Harold in romantic scenes with Karla (Ellie Valleau). It looked like I might have to rethink the casting until Arthur Mendoza suggested H.M. Wynant, the husband of one of his former acting students.

I reached out to H.M., sent him the play, and we decided to meet for lunch at Astro Burger on the edge of Glendale. "I tried everything to not do it. But how could I?" recalled H.M. "It was an enormous role. I never leave the stage! How could I say no?"

The play opened on October 20, 1994 at Mendoza's 47-seat, equity-waver theater and had an eight-week run. Neither H.M. nor anyone else in the eight-person cast ever missed a performance. What I marveled at most of all was H.M.'s precision, night after night. When we shot the production on video over three nights, from three different angles, the editor could match-cut from one performance to the next on H.M.'s physical turns and hand gestures, which were always on the exact same lines in every performance.

The play would ultimately be awarded a Drama-Logue Critics Award for Outstanding Achievement in Writing at a ceremony at the Pasadena Playhouse, where Ethel had been a student in the early 1950's alongside Ed Asner. It is currently published by Samuel French / Concord Theatricals.

A year later, James McManus, who had played Bill in *Karlaboy*, wrote a role specifically for H.M. in an independently financed, contemporary film noir, *The Big Empty*, to be directed by his NYU Film School classmate, Jack Perez. McManus cast himself in the lead as Lloyd, an inept, novice private eye. At one point, Lloyd gets in a little too deep with his case on a personal level and seeks the counsel of his PI mentor, J.W. McCreedy (H.M.). It's a long, terrific scene and gave H.M. quite a lot to do. It may be one of his most naturalistic performances. The film was released in 1997 and won Best Screenplay at the AFI Film Festival. But without a proper talent agent nor manager soliciting work for him, it would be six years before H.M. acted again for Film or TV.

It would have seemed an opportune time for H.M. to resume his sculpting, but such was not the case: "I stopped sculpting after my second divorce. It's not easy working in marble. It's hard work. Also, you have to have the space to do it and I don't have a proper studio now (in the Valley Glen home) so it's very difficult."

During this period, H.M. performed a few fun roles in 99-seat equity waiver stage productions, most notably, as Mervyn in veteran stage director Jules Aaron's production of Wendy Wasserstein's *The Sisters Rosensweig* at Century Playhouse in October 1998, and as philandering family patriarch Seth Lord in an April 2000 production of *The Philadelphia Story* by Philip Barry at the Court Theater, starring Alison Eastwood (Clint's daughter) as H.M.'s daughter.

But the real "live production" that 73-year-old H.M. had undertaken a year earlier was not in a theater at all but back at home where 44-year-old Paula was pregnant with their child. H.M. had had a vasectomy decades earlier and that, coupled, with Paula's age, made IVF the only choice. The notion of becoming a father at such an advanced age was not H.M.'s idea and, in fact, he was terrified at the prospect. But Paula knew what she wanted and was an immoveable force, running the show beginning in early 1999, doing all the research, and making the finances work.

The couple was told they had less than a 5% chance of conceiving, but after the couple's very first IVF attempt in the Fall of '99, the pregnancy was successful. H.M.'s first daughter, Pasha

H.M. and Paula with their toddler, Pasha, named after
H.M.'s mother, in a 2002 family portrait.

Chapter Eighteen

NEW CENTURY, NEW WORK (2001-Present)

Working for his oldest son and for his biggest fans

"It's the most unusual thing that ever happened in my life. Having a female child. I loved it."

Back in the 1950's and '60's, when H.M. raised his three boys, he was constantly working and had live-in help Monday through Friday. This time around at fatherhood, Paula was working 40 hours per week and H.M. became the exclusive daytime parent for the first time in his life. And to a daughter!

The good news was that despite his great resistance to the IVF process back in 1999, despite waking from sweat-drenched, panic-soaked nightmares and asking the pregnant Paula, "What the hell are we doing?!", despite all the fear… H.M. took to fatherhood at this time of life with great joy. He delighted in raising Pasha, driving her to and from school, preparing her meals, and doing home chores. He had had a great run on Broadway, Film, and TV. Now it was time for a quiet family life, uninterrupted by the work grind.

As Pasha, now 24, echoed, "He was an amazing Dad when I was growing up. He helped me a lot with school projects, making crazy sculptures for my presentations. He even made a camera out of cardboard for one class project. I used to drive him nuts making him play card games with me over and over, like Crazy Eights and Go Fish."

As a little girl, when Pasha showed an interest in performing, H.M. and Paula were encouraging but never pushed her. "They helped me but always made sure I took the time to do it right," recalled Pasha.

In her early teens, Pasha grew less interested in performing. "At fifteen, I fell in love with the technical side of Theatre — lighting, construction," Pasha elaborated. "Dad was thrilled about it. He'd give me advice and tell me all about having done the very same work building the Richard Basehart Playhouse."

This new chapter of being a caretaker not only meant tending to his growing daughter… but also his first wife, Ethel.

After she had left NBC as an executive, Ethel became a producer of movies and miniseries, primarily working with John Frankenheimer, with whom she had worked as far back as his *Playhouse 90* days. She was an Executive Producer on his TNT miniseries *Andersonville* in '96 (in which Bruce had a supporting role) which garnered seven Emmy nominations and a win for Frankenheimer as director. In 1999, she was inducted into the Television Hall of Fame, but by 2002 (age 80), she was in poor health and slowing down considerably, having only a Consultant credit on Frankenheimer's HBO film that year, *Path to War*.

By this point, oldest son William was firmly entrenched in Northern California as a musician, composer, and teacher. Youngest son Bruce had left Los Angeles for the East Coast, where he was having a successful acting career, touring in Broadway productions of *Les Misérables* and *Ragtime*, among others, as well as raising a family. Unfortunately, Ethel and her one Los Angeles-based son, Scott, never reconciled the hurts and indignities he had suffered over the perception that Ethel was not only anti-nepotism, but had actually made efforts to hinder Scott's success.

So, after a lifetime of brilliantly managing CBS and NBC, but poorly managing both her finances and children, Ethel found herself broke, unable to live on her own, and with none of her sons able to swoop in to save her. She moved into the Motion Picture Home in Woodland Hills with the assistance of her closest family — H.M. and Paula.

Aided by Paula, who had always had a good relationship with Ethel, H.M. took her to all her doctor's appointments, fed her cats, shopped for her. H.M.'s recollection of Ethel's final years gets him teary eyed for the only time in our interview sessions, "At the end, I gave her ALL of me. I intimately gave her everything. All my love. I was with her right 'til the bloody end."

Ethel Winant passed away at the Motion Picture Home on

November 29, 2003 at the age of 81. H.M. and Paula took in Ethel's cat, Sonoma, who remained a part of their household for eleven more years.

Afterward, regardless of having no agent nor manager, work still managed to find its way to H.M.

First up was a role from his son Scott, who had developed into a heavy-hitter TV Executive Producer and Director, beginning with his breakthrough as a Producer and then Director on the hit ABC series, *Thirtysomething* (1987-1991). *My So-Called Life* followed (also on ABC), but it was Scott's creative association with TV's hit Aaron Sorkin series, *The West Wing*, that in 2003, got H.M. his first network television role in nine years, in the Season Five episode, "Jefferson Lives". He portrayed one of a half-dozen senators who are being interviewed for the Vice President position. In the finished product, it appeared as if H.M.'s scene was trimmed heavily. He goes into a room to be interviewed and then is barely seen. Still, it was a new network credit on a high-profile show and likely, a decent paycheck.

The next year gave 77-year-old H.M. a juicier scene on Scott's new Showtime series *Huff*, starring Hank Azaria as a psychiatrist with a few psychological problems of his own. In the Season One episode, "All the King's Horses", H.M., playing the angry husband of one of Huff's older female patients (Bonnie Bartlett), asks for time with Huff because he thinks his wife is only learning one thing in therapy: "how to hate me faster." Directed by Martha Coolidge (*Valley Girl*), H.M. gave the sort of focused, grounded, un-showy performance that should have gotten him more career traction, but such efforts require an effective agent or manager, neither of which H.M. had.

Although H.M. did not have any on-screen credits in 2005, he was presented with an opportunity when Christopher Caliendo, the composer of the incidental score to *Karlaboy*, the stage play H.M. had starred in in 1994, found himself working with cult independent filmmaker, Larry Blamire. Blamire had gotten on the map when his ingenious valentine to low budget 1950's sci-fi B movies, *The Lost Skeleton of Cadavra*, caught the eye of Sony Pictures' Vice President of Repertory and Acquisitions (and also a ravenous film historian), Michael Schlesinger, at a film festival in the early 2000's.

Schlesinger was largely in charge of maintaining the studio's vast archive of Columbia Pictures library titles, supervising their journey to DVD and Blu-Ray, and in some cases, the restoration and re-release of certain library titles into first run theaters. Nevertheless, he loved *Lost Skeleton*, and while new first run films were not typical his purview at Sony, he was able to make the case to the powers that be that for very little money, they could take a shot on Blamire's Zucker Brothers-type inspired lunacy, resulting in a 2004 limited theatrical release.

Thanks to that cache, Blamire was able to raise funds for three independently produced films in a row, the first being *Trail of the Screaming Forehead*. Along with writing, directing, and acting, Blamire had penned a theme song, gotten Manhattan Transfer to agree to perform it, and hired Caliendo to write the music and produce the opening tune. Blamire was lamenting to Caliendo how he was still in search of an old-time character actor to play his main villain, Dr. Applethorpe. Discussions with Martin Landau for the role had fallen through when Landau got booked in a TV series. Caliendo, who had grown friendly with H.M. and Paula, asked if Larry knew who H.M. Wynant was. Blamire, a longtime fan and historian of both big screen and small-screen Westerns (as well as *Perry Mason*) knew H.M.'s work thoroughly.

"You really know H.M. Wynant?!" Blamire asked Caliendo, in awe. He did, indeed.

H.M. and Blamire met at the Magnolia Grill and H.M. agreed to play the role. Taking place in the fictitious town of Longhead Bay, *Trail of the Screaming Forehead* involves an invasion of alien forehead creatures that descend en masse using H.M.'s Dr. Applethorpe as their instrument. At the same time, local scientist Dr. Sheila Bexter (Fay Masterson) is conducting experiments based on her theory that human intelligence is stored in the forehead. To prove this, she creates "foreheadazine" and tests the serum on her unsuspecting colleague, Dr. Latham (Andrew Parks) after which, things spin out of control, and the town is faced with a cataclysm of epic proportions.

According to Blamire, H.M. couldn't have been more professional and polished by the time cameras finally rolled in October and November of 2006, never having any problems with what Blamire himself describes as his "sometimes deliberately overripe dialogue."

One of the delights for Blamire was hiring veteran actor, James Karen (*Return of the Living Dead*), in one of the smaller villain roles because, as Blamire recalled, "H and Jimmy had never met before, but they realized that their careers and all the people they knew, paralleled absolutely to a tee, it tracked. They knew all the same people, and their careers took a similar course and yet they never met before. It was fascinating to hear them shooting the breeze."

"I try to have a happy set," Blamire explained. "H contributed to that. You hear his laughter. He loved to laugh. It was obvious he was having a good time."

"There was a pool table at the wrap party. My favorite image of the night was H running the table, chewing gum. He was

Getting to exercise his comedy chops as Dr. Applethorpe in Larry Blamire's *Trail of the Screaming Forehead*. Pictured with Andrew Parks.

Rare glimpse at the ace pool player, which began when H.M. was a bad boy in Detroit. From the *Screaming Forehead* wrap party. Photo courtesy of Larry Blamire.

playing one of the crew members. It was the coolest thing I'd ever seen."

Something that still moves Blamire to this day is H.M.'s inscription on his *Screaming Forehead* poster: "Larry - You changed my life. Best Always, H.M." This was not an empty inscription. H.M. truly felt that having such a significant role in a feature film (something he hadn't had for ten years), with such a fun, appreciative team at the helm, gave him a new optimism for the road ahead.

While Blamire was waiting for the film's 2007 limited release, he wrote and directed a series of *Twilight Zone*-ish absurdist comedy shorts under the series title, *Tales from the Pub*, utilizing the little mini-tavern a friend had built in his basement. Viewable on YouTube, H.M. played Eton Trent in the episode "Puppet for Your Thoughts", in which a Puppet Vendor (Kevin Quinn) is determined to sell Eton a puppet he does not want… or does he? It is arguably the best episode, no small thanks to H.M.'s all-in performance. "His gravity made that work," Blamire insisted. "He knew to approach it very seriously. The more affronted he is by this vendor, the funnier it is."

Early in the year, H.M. was delightfully blindsided when Paula and friends took over a nearby Italian restaurant and threw H.M. a surprise 80th birthday party. M.C.'d by the author, Blamire was among the guests as was Oscar-winner Margaret O'Brien (*Meet Me In Saint Louis, Little Women*). Eighty-two-year-old comedian Shelley Berman (*Curb Your Enthusiasm*) delivered a monologue in tribute to H.M. that left everyone in stitches. Paula had a touching career clip-reel created and capped the party by presenting H.M. with a Rolex watch to replace the one he had lost, which had been gifted to him by Elvis Presley.

Summer of '07 brought H.M. and I together professionally again, so I will resume first-person for a moment. At this point in my career, I had had a major screenwriting credit, having written the screenplay adaptation of my stage play, *The Cat's Meow*, for a film directed by Peter Bogdanovich and starring Kirsten Dunst, Eddie Izzard, Edward Herrmann, Carey Elwes, and Jennifer Tilly, involving a murder on board William Randolph Hearst's yacht.

After the film's release in 2002 by Lionsgate, I began working with three sets of producers on three different movies to be my feature directing debut. As each project reached frustrating snags, I was challenged by my girlfriend at the time (actress, Sybil Temtchine) to make a movie for an amount of money I could raise rather than an amount I couldn't. And so, my feature directorial debut, *Footprints*, was born.

Taking place from sunrise to sunset, and shot entirely on and around Hollywood Boulevard, it involves a young, unnamed woman (Temtchine) who awakens at dawn, lying on the footprints of Grauman's Chinese with no idea who she is or how she got there. Throughout the course of the day, she is handed off from one iconic boulevard denizen to the next (tour bus drivers, superhero impersonators, Scientology auditor, etc.), all leading to the revelation of her identity.

Shot over seven days in the summer of 2007 for $38,000, the schedule necèssitated that the actors learn and rehearse the text like a stage play (often rehearsing at the actual Hollywood Boulevard locations), shooting their scenes in extended takes. I wrote several of the roles for people I knew, including the male lead role of Victor for H.M., an elegant, older gentleman, sporting a bolo tie, who's interest in the lost young woman we suspect is based on more than simple charity. Even Paula and 7-year-old Pasha got into the act for a brief, but meaningful moment of screen time.

H.M. gave a performance that is at once sensitive, mysterious, compelling, and inherently informed by his own Hollywood history of triumph and tragedy. It was his suggestion to softly sing the song "Daisy" at a key moment, which resulted in one of the film's most touching moments.

During its road to distribution, the film was championed by directors Curtis Hanson (*L.A. Confidential*) and Monte Hellman (*Two Lane Blacktop*), who both offered quotes of endorsement, as

As Victor, who may or may not be aiding the amnesiac young woman (Sybil Temtchine) in the independent film, *Footprints*, shot on Hollywood Boulevard.

Between takes with writer/director Larry Blamire on the set of *Dark and Stormy Night*. Photo courtesy of Larry Blamire.

did legendary Cannes Film Festival advisor and tastemaker, Pierre Rissient, who made efforts to have *Footprints* included in the "Un Certain Regard" section of the festival, but it was not to be.

Between shooting *Footprints* in 2007 and the film's distribution, H.M. appeared in two more features for Larry Blamire which both found financing at the same time. The first was *The Lost Skeleton Returns Again* (shot in March 2008 and released in 2009), the writer/director's sequel to his debut feature. The cast of the first film was reassembled for a trip up the Amazon. And since two of the leads were killed in the first film, naturally they appeared in the sequel as the deceased's identical twin brother(s).

Blamire so enjoyed working with H.M. on *Forehead* and *Tales from the Pub* that he wrote a very funny, curtain-raising role just for him: General Scottmanson, the sort of thoughtful, but no-nonsense military man found in 1950's sci-fi films. H.M. is so pitch-perfect in his delivery, and gets so many laughs, that one only wishes he had appeared throughout the rest of the film. Blamire himself realized this and was planning to expand General Scottmanson's role greatly in a third *Lost Skeleton* film, but alas, financing has yet to come through.

The entire company rolled into the next film, an "Old Dark House" sendup called *Dark and Stormy Night*, shot entirely in black and white in the Summer of 2008. Cast as Dr. Van Von

Vandervon, H.M. is a psychiatrist from a nearby mental institution with slicked hair and ripe monologues who mysteriously skirts the periphery of both the story and the old, dark house until finally ringing the doorbell. His hands-off philosophy to taking care of the criminally insane leaves much to be desired since he can't recall the name, gender, nor physical description of the escaped madman… or madwoman, who just may be killing off those gathered in the house, one by one.

As with all his work for Blamire, and earlier still in *Get Smart*, *Hogan's Heroes*, and *The Doris Day Show*, H.M. was clearly adept at comedy, knowing the best way to get a laugh was to play it straight.

After the Shout! Factory releases of both of Blamire's 2009 films, *Footprints* premiered at the Starz Denver Film Festival in 2009 and was invited to Method Fest next, where H.M. was nominated for Best Supporting Actor by the jury. The film was released by Paladin in New York and Los Angeles in April 2011 with a Los Angeles premiere at Grauman's Chinese. At age 84, it was H.M.'s first premiere at the Chinese in a starring role.

In his glowing, literate, and in-depth review in the New York Press, critic Armond White (then President of the New York Film Critics Circle) said of H.M., "He has a Peckinpah face—like William Holden's or Gig Young's— of youth in desuetude, lined with experience." Two months later, when White subsequently listed *Footprints* among his Top Ten Films in his mid-year report, the endorsement aided in having the film booked into theaters in Phoenix, Albuquerque, Buffalo, and San Francisco, where critic Mick LaSalle championed it with a rave review in the San Francisco Chronicle.

Also in the cast, and delivering a touching performance (nominated for Best Supporting Actress at Method Fest), was Pippa Scott (*Auntie Mame, The Searchers*) who had co-starred with H.M. in the 1967 episode of *I Spy* entitled, "Apollo".

In a fitting coda, Blamire's champion and sometimes producer, Michael Schlesinger, reached out to H.M. for his own directorial debut — a series of five 20-25 minute comedy shorts, shot as if made in the 1930's or 40's,

Paula and H.M. at the red carpet premiere of *Footprints* at Grauman's Chinese Theater, April 13, 2011. The actor's first premiere at the Chinese in a starring role.

starring a fictitious comedy duo named Biffle and Shooster, played respectively by Nick Santa Maria and Will Ryan who had created the characters.

Shot in 2014, H.M. starred in Schlesinger's *The Biffle Murder Case* as Andrew, the patriarch to a family of ne'er-do-wells and leeches. When one of his sons is murdered, enter police Lt. Frank Murphy (Robert Forster) to crack the case (spoiler alert: H.M.'s the mad killer). Shot on sets built at Remmet Studios in Canoga Park when H.M. was 87-years-old, to date, it is his last major appearance on the big or small screen. All five Biffle and Shooster comedy shorts were released as one collection on DVD by Kino Lorber.

That same year, on August 14, 2014, H.M. received a Life-

Off camera clowning with comedy team Biffle (Nick Santa Maria) and Shooster (Will Ryan) in *The Biffle Murder Case*. Photo courtesy of writer/director, Michael Schlesinger.

H.M. accepting his Lifetime Achievement award at Cinecon. Photo courtesy of Stan Taffel.

Posing with fellow recipients of the Cinecon Lifetime Achievement Award at Hollywood's Loews Hotel. From left: Ruta Lee, Barbara Luna, and Francine York. Cinecon's Bob Birchard in background. Photo courtesy of Stan Taffel.

time Achievement Award at the 50th Cinecon Classic Film Festival, presented to him by Festival President, Stan Taffel, at a ceremony at the Loews Hotel in Hollywood. Cinecon, which screens films largely from the silent era through the 1940's, has operated every year on Labor Day weekend since 1964.

In the ten years since that award and his participation in the writing of this book, H.M. (97 as of this writing), continues to live a quiet life, enjoying his four dogs, drives to the beach, books, friends, and of course, his family. At an age when most have ceased to travel, H.M. has no problem hopping in the car, as he did this year, to witness and celebrate his daughter Pasha's graduation ceremony from UC Irvine with a degree in Environmental Engineering.

He continues to give interviews, answer fan mail, and up until very recently, drive his vintage Jaguar. Aided only by a walking stick — which H.M. himself carved from a single piece of wood — he

Recent photo of H.M. and three of his four children: Pasha, Scott, and Bruce.

attended The Hollywood Show at the Marriott Hotel in Burbank, California, in June of 2024 where he was not only asked for autographs from longtime fans, but discovered by new young fans who had no idea this man — who had starred in *The Twilight Zone*, *Batman*, the *Planet of the Apes* saga, and had fought dirty with Elvis — was still alive and kicking. He may very well have been the oldest celebrity that weekend and it clearly meant a lot to those in attendance.

"Who is that *old man*?!" H.M. will often say when he sees photos of himself or looks in the mirror. It's Hyman Oscar Weiner a.k.a. Haim Winant a.k.a. H.M. Wynant, who wanted no more out of life than to be a steadily working actor.

Well, given this was the wish of a man who aced four episodes of *Mission: Impossible* — Mission: Accomplished!

9 798887 715742